Thank You!

The content in this curriculum has been inspired by the core values of Bethel Church in Redding, California, as well as Dann Farrelly's book *Kingdom Culture: Living the Values That Disciple Nations,* which can be purchased from the Bethel website: **shop.bethel.com**

We also would like to acknowledge the Bethel Children's team that
helped make this curriculum possible:
Amy Gagnon
Bea Ryan
Diana Daugherty
Candace Kazynski
Yilin Munoz
Andrew Liem
Josiah Higgins

Cover design by Martin Hofer & Muster Creative.
Layout design by Muster Creative.
Produced by Bethel Children's Ministry & Enliven Media.

Printed in the United States.

ISBN 13 TP: 978-0-7684-5802-2
ISBN 13 eBook: 978-0-7684-5804-6

Table of Contents

Introduction 4

Testimonies 5

Before You Get Started. 6

Lesson Overview 7

Lesson 1: Intro into Kingdom Core Values. 15

Lesson 2: God Is Good 21

Lesson 3: Salvation Creates Joyful Identity. 29

Lesson 4: Responsive to Grace. 37

Lesson 5: Focused on His Presence 45

Lesson 6: Creating Healthy Family 51

Lesson 7: God's Word Transforms 59

Lesson 8: God Is Still Speaking 67

Lesson 9: Jesus Empowers Supernatural Ministry 75

Lesson 10: His Kingdom Is Advancing. 83

Lesson 11: Free and Responsible. 91

Lesson 12: Honor Affirms Value 99

Lesson 13: Generous like Our Father 107

Lesson 14: Hope in a Glorious Church. 115

Conclusion. 122

Appendix 123

Introduction

Children's Ministry at Bethel Church is driven by the belief that there is no junior Holy Spirit. Children at any age can walk in a relationship with God in all His expressions. Our desire is that children know their identity in Jesus, see themselves as carriers of His Spirit, and therefore have been given all authority to do what was commanded in the Great Commission.

We are so excited to go on this journey with you! We believe you will discover God's core thoughts toward you and the children you work with as you explore each lesson. This curriculum was developed to start building foundational core beliefs in our children. The lessons in this series are targeted for first through fourth grade, however, they could be adapted for a younger or older audience as needed.

One of our team's core beliefs is, "what feeds you, feeds others." Therefore, as you study these lessons we encourage you and your team to first seek what the Lord has for you before teaching to the children. Let it become real for you and let the Lord encounter you through these lessons. Every child deserves an encounter with their Creator, the one who adores and knows them inside and out.

As you take and apply these lessons, you will see identity and purpose come alive in you, your team, and all the children you work with. We pray this foundation is only the beginning of what God will build in and through you and your ministry. Thank you for investing into God's kingdom and growing the next generation. They are the future leaders who WILL change the world.

We're excited for you to go on this journey with us!

Blessings to you,

Testimonies

Revelation 20:19 says, "The testimony of Jesus is the spirit of prophecy." Bethel highly values sharing testimonies for two reasons:

1. We love getting to celebrate what God has done and thanking Him.
2. The word testimony means "do it again." Every time we share what God has done, it is an invitation for you to see God do this within your church and children's ministry.

Here are just a couple of testimonies we want to share. We encourage you to be expectant to see God do great things over the next fourteen weeks.

Hunger for Scripture

Many of our children come from churched backgrounds but without much personal knowledge of scripture. Throughout the weeks of Bible memorization games and challenges, many of the children gained a new value and appreciation for scripture and even felt more comfortable finding, memorizing, and applying scripture to their lives. One of our children even began using his Bible to speak out prophetic words and call out what God was doing in both the room and at home!

Word of Knowledge Healing

One day we had a child get a word of knowledge for another child in the room. The room proceeded to pray for the child, and she got healed! The child who was healed then found out that one of the leaders in the room also had the same problem, prayed for her, and she got healed too!

Love of Bobbie

We found that the children loved Bobbie Baker so much that on days when we had other lessons scheduled, the children would constantly ask where Bobbie was! They loved when Bobbie shared and often remembered little details about Bobbie that surprised us. We love that Bobbie so effectively demonstrated the core values to our children so that they are growing up reflecting kingdom core values.

Before You Get Started

Setting Up Your Room

We have found it best to divide the children by the grade level. To do this we lay down rectangular, cloth mats of different colors, one color for each grade.

For example:
- First grade has a red mat
- Second grade has a green mat
- Third grade has a blue mat
- Fourth grade has a yellow mat

For smaller rooms, you may want to have one mat for first and second grade and one mat for third and fourth grade. By using the designated mats, your children always know where to sit when they come in the room, which helps them to feel safe, know which group is theirs every week, and allows them to build connection with others around their same age.

Gathering Supplies

At the beginning of each lesson, you will find a supply list with the items you need for that lesson so that you are able to be prepped and ready before you start each day. Prepping all of these supplies beforehand will set you up for success and allows you to give your attention to leading and feeling fully present with the children in your service.

Supplies Needed for Every Lesson:

- Two-part, tear-off carnival tickets
- Container to keep tickets (We suggest a baker's hat)
- Folder to keep all your Bible memorization charts in and empty charts for new children
- Two-minute "Ticket Timer"
- Equipment to play the videos of Bobbie Baker, if you choose to use the videos for the lesson
- Bobbie Baker's costume (baker's hat, mustache, and apron), if you decide to teach the Bobbie part of the lessons live

Lesson Overview

These lessons are designed to help you make your classroom a place where God can encounter your children rather than it just being a daycare. Each lesson was developed so that your children are learning about God in a corporate setting just like their parents. We have found that our youngest people experience God in powerful ways at church. It has been a fun and exciting journey to bring a whole family vibrancy from church into their homes.

Each lesson has an identifiable rhythm and structure. Children thrive in repetition, structure, and knowing what to expect when they enter your room. If you find that an element falls in a better order for your particular service, feel free to move it, but keep it the same for all of the following weeks. When your children understand the flow of your room, this also helps them to know what is expected behaviorally for the day.

Within each lesson there is journaling space to customize your day or write down any creative ideas you have.

Lesson Outline

- **Greet Children**
- **Connect Time** 10 minutes
- **Bible Memorization Game** 30 minutes
- **Teaching** 15 minutes
- **Bobbie Baker** 5 minutes
- **Activation** 10 minutes
- **Tickets & Treasure Box** 5 minutes
- **End Game** 25 minutes
- **Goodbye**

Find detailed descriptions on the following pages.

GREETING CHILDREN

Always greet each child as they enter the room. Do this by getting at eye level with each child, saying their name, and welcoming them to your room. If you are excited for the children to be part of your room, they will be excited to be there! Children feeling seen and known by you and other leaders builds a necessary connection.

Try to connect with the parents at the door, letting them know what you are planning for the day. Possibly the theme or the Bible lesson story.

CONNECT TIME 10 minutes

Purpose

Connect time is one of the most important parts of the day because it provides a time for the children to feel comfortable as they transition from their family into your room. Over time, you will see how important this part of the day is. It can be a vital part of your investing in children.

Description

As children are entering into your classroom there will be a game to provide more connection between all of the children. You'll continue to play this game until you have the majority of your children gathered in one location.

Once most of your children have joined your room, let the children know you will be transitioning to the next activity which will be the Bible memorization game.

BIBLE MEMORIZATION GAME 30 minutes

Purpose

Bible memorization is a vital part of this curriculum because it allows your children to learn how powerful and fun it can be to learn scripture. This also makes space for the child to have one-on-one interaction with a leader as they are reciting their verse, which ensures that every child has a moment to connect personally with their leaders. All of the Bible verses that will be memorized relate to the kingdom core value the children will be learning on that day.

Description

During the Bible memorization game, there will be a unique way the children are learning the scripture for each week. Have all the children gather as one large group and play until

the majority of children are able to memorize the verse. You will then have the children recite the verse they just learned with a designated leader in your room. Keep the game going through this time so that the children have the opportunity to play the game again to remember the verse a bit better.

You may have children who come to the leader to say the verse, but they do not know the verse completely. Have them return to the main game to learn the verse a bit better, and then return to recite the verse again. Give them a few chances at reciting the verse because they may think they had memorized it, but did not know it as well as they thought.

Give the children a warning when you are about a minute away from closing the time they can recite the scripture. Hold a standard of the children saying the whole verse before considering it memorized and getting a prize. We want these verses to be remembered in their brains, but more importantly in their hearts!

BIBLE MEMORIZATION CHART

Purpose

Tracking the verses memorized throughout the curriculum will give your children the best sense of accomplishment at the end of the curriculum. When they can look back and see all that they have learned, they will be impressed with themselves and excited to share with their family as well!

Description

Each child will have their own chart to track their memorized verses. You can make copies of the Bible Memorization Chart in the Appendix. Make a few extra copies for children who are guests that day. To mark the verses that are memorized, we suggest using mustache stickers that look like Bobbie's mustache or gold star stickers.

Once the child has memorized the verse, have them go to where you are keeping the charts and put their sticker on for the week. The leader may want to hold on to the folder so they can see children put their stickers on as this is another opportunity to affirm each child individually.

REWARD SYSTEM FOR MEMORIZING SCRIPTURE

Purpose

The reward system is a great incentive for the children to learn the Bible verses and for them to persevere on the weeks that have a more complicated verse to learn.

Description

There are several ways you can do rewards each time a child memorizes a verse. For younger children, giving them a prize directly after saying the verse correctly will increase the engagement level during this activity. We suggest using the same prize every week for this part of the lesson, for example, a lollipop.

Have only one choice available for a reward which will save you the extra time it takes for children to choose from multiple prizes. For example, red lollipops for one service and maybe blue for the following week. We do this because having each child recite a verse individually will take a good amount of time.

If you have some older children, you may want to let them build up to a grand prize. Let them know that if they are able to completely fill out their chart by the last week, they will get a gift card, toy, or king-size candy bar.

TEACHING 10-15 minutes

Purpose

During this time you have the opportunity to reinforce the heart of the kingdom core value you are teaching that week. You are also are making sure each child is understanding the content and looking for an opportunity for deeper spiritual conversation. Asking engaging questions throughout the lesson often helps them to keep their brains turned on and involved in the content.

Description

All of the teachings for the individual lessons are provided. The goal is not to read from the page, but to learn the main points of the teachings and to put your own heart into the topic each week. We recommend going through the lesson and spending about thirty minutes to add any notes you have to customize it for your classroom.

The more comfortable and engaged you are with the content, the more the children will be interested and excited about what is being taught. We suggest assigning different parts of the lesson to your team who are willing to teach. This allows your team to grow in confidence and authority in your service and with your children.

INCORPORATING BOBBIE BAKER 5 minutes

Purpose

Bobbie is designed to take big concepts and turn them into fun and simple tools that children can remember later. He will take all of the kingdom core values and use different cooking ingredients in each lesson that will point the children back to God and His truths in each lesson.

Description

There are two ways that you can use Bobbie Baker in your lessons.

Option 1: Have one member of your team be Bobbie Baker for each lesson and have him teach live in the room. You will need:
- His signature baker's hat, apron, mustache, and Bible as "recipe book"
- The same person playing him every time
  - On weeks that person cannot be there, introduce the person taking his place as a sibling or cousin of Bobbie
    Example: "Hi everyone, Bobbie could not be here today, but he sent me in his place. My name is Brody. I am Bobbie's sister/brother/cousin…"
- Have the person who dresses up as Bobbie change clothes where the children cannot see to keep the illusion

Option 2: Use our videos of Bobbie Baker which can either be accessed through:
- The flash drive with your physical curriculum
- The digital download

ACTIVATION 10 minutes

Purpose

The activation section is a time where you are activating the children in whatever you are teaching on in the lesson. Activation happens through prayer, personal encounter, or prophetic acts. We believe that when children are marked by the Holy Spirit during these encounters, they will carry these experiences throughout their lives and know God in a very personal way.

Description

Every lesson that includes an activation gives you specific instructions for how to carry out these activities. During this time you will be imparting a kingdom core value to the children by having them connect to Holy Spirit. Have high expectations during this time that God will

speak to the children and impact them in a significant way. It is always a good idea to allow the children to share with you what they experienced after these times.

A key to making this time successful on the days when your children may be having higher energy is by ensuring you have the attention of the children before you start the activation. To do this have the children all posture themselves in the same way, whether sitting or standing, and have them connect to the Holy Spirit. A great way to have them feel connected to Holy Spirit is to have them close their eyes, put their hand on their heart, and say all together, "Holy Spirit fill me with your peace." After this, have the children raise their hands when they feel connected to the Holy Spirit's peace, and then continue on with the activation planned for the day.

TICKETS & TREASURE BOX TOOL 5 minutes

Note: If you already have a classroom management tool in place, you can continue using it for consistency during this time. Here is an optional easy and effective tool we use.

Purpose

Tickets and the use of a treasure box are given to children to keep their attention and raise their level of engagement during the lesson and activities. It helps with behavior as children earn tickets if they are honoring others and are following whatever established rules you have for your particular service.

- For the container which holds tickets, we suggest using a baker's hat.
- For the timer use an egg timer, your cell phone, or look up a two-minute timer online.
- The treasure box prizes are different than the prizes the children are getting for Bible memorization. A "treasure box" is a box filled with different kinds of prizes that children can choose from when redeeming their tickets. Some suggestions are: fidget spinners, puzzles, fun stickers, candy, slime in a container, or anything fun that your children feel especially excited about.

Description

- To use this ticket system you will need a roll of two-part carnival tickets.
- Tear off one part of the ticket and give to the child, and then put the other part into some kind of container to pull from later. **Note:** Both parts of the ticket have the same numbers on them.
- Only give tickets out to children who are following directions, participating, and not distracting others.
- During the "ticket timer" part of the lesson, you will have a two-minute timer that counts down as you pull tickets, during which time you pull as many tickets as possible.
- Have either a leader or a child pull the ticket number from the baker's hat. The child whose number is called gets to pull a prize from the treasure box.

Note: Children have to be completely silent for the leader to pull tickets, even if the time runs out completely.

Remove all of the tickets from the hat at the end of every service so that children are not able to keep their tickets for multiple weeks. Having too many tickets can be overwhelming for children. We recommend a child receives no more than three tickets in a given service.

END GAME 25 minutes

Purpose

The end game is a great time for the children to get their extra energy out, build connection with the other children, and simply have a lot of fun!

Description

These games can be lead by an adult leader or by children who are in your room. These games are designed to wrap up your service and give you something to do as parents are picking up the children. Some of these games will rotate throughout the curriculum so that your children become familiar with them and get excited to play the games they know.

SAYING GOODBYE

When children are leaving for the day, this is a good time to say goodbye to each child and connect with parents. Tell them a little bit about something good that happened with their child during the service.

Example: "Jesus showed Jane a really cool picture today that was really powerful. I think it may be for your family. Make sure to ask her about it on your way home."

Lesson 1
Intro into Kingdom Core Values

Supply List for Every Lesson

- ☐ Carnival tickets
- ☐ Container (baker's hat) for tickets
- ☐ Folder with Bible memorization charts
- ☐ Blank memorization charts for new children
- ☐ Stickers for chart completion
- ☐ Two-minute ticket timer
- ☐ Bobbie Baker
- ☐ Video and something to the play the video
  Or
- ☐ Live Skit with Bobbie's costume and props

Supply List for Lesson 1

- ☐ Ball or object to throw for game
- ☐ Giant paper with verse written out
- ☐ Post-It Notes to cover words
  Or
- ☐ Whiteboard with marker and eraser with the verse written out
- ☐ Bobbie Baker props (if doing live skit):
  - ☐ Chef hat
  - ☐ Mustache
  - ☐ Apron
  - ☐ Recipe book "Bible"
  - ☐ Giant cookie to eat OR cake batter in bowl
  - ☐ Wooden spoon or whisk to taste the batter
  - ☐ Picture of fancy cake in a fancy frame

Main Themes

For this lesson we will be letting the children know about what they can expect throughout the course of these lessons. We will break down kingdom core values and also introduce Bobbie Baker to the children. The tone you set with this lesson will carry on for the weeks to come.

CONNECT TIME 10 minutes

Have children learn each other's names by sitting in a circle and throwing a ball (or object) to each other across the circle. When the children catch it, they have to say their name and the name of the person who threw it.

If the children know each other already, have the children say their favorite food and the favorite food of the person who went before them. Once you have ten children in a circle, start a new circle so children do not have too many names to learn and remember.

If you have time, you could mix up the circles after a while so the children can learn about more children in the service.

BIBLE MEMORIZATION 30 minutes

John 3:16

God so loved the world that He gave His one and only Son. Anyone who believes in Him will not die but will have eternal life. (NIRV)

GAME: ERASER GAME 30 minutes

Have the verse written on a giant paper or whiteboard and erase one word at a time.

- Have the children read the whole verse together three times before you start erasing words.
- Each time you erase a word, the children have to read the whole verse again, and remember the words that are missing. You can erase words in any order you want.
- Follow this order until all the words are gone, and have the children recite the verse all the way through. After a few words are erased, celebrate the children for how well they have done so far and encourage them to keep going!

GAME: ERASER GAME (Continued)

- As soon as you have erased the majority of the words, you can have the children line up behind a leader who is ready to hear their verse. For those children who need a bit more time memorizing, start the game over for them.
- Have the leader listening to the verses stand far enough away from the game being played so they are not hearing the verse being said during the game.
- Once the children think they know the verse, they can go to the designated leader to share.
- If they remember the verse, give them the prize; if they have forgotten, have the child return to the group to practice the verse.
  - This is also the time where they get to put their sticker on their Bible memorization chart.

TEACHING INTRO 5 minutes

Let the children know they will be learning about kingdom core values and talk about Bobbie Baker. Let them know they will get to meet him soon!

- **Welcome, everyone! For the next fourteen weeks, we are going to be focusing on kingdom core values.**
- **We are going to be have lots of fun memorizing scripture, and for every verse you remember you can earn prizes.**
- **This year, you will learn why we as Christians believe what we believe; and through these core values, you will learn how you can change the world!**
- **When you learn these values, you will be transformed, see miracles, healings, and be changed from the inside out!**
- **Now, I want to introduce you to someone who will be with us while we learn about the core values every week. His name is Bobbie Baker and he loves the kingdom core values. He is going to show us how, when all the ingredients in core values work together, they make something heavenly.**

BOBBIE BAKER 5 minutes

Bobbie will help break down the kingdom core value and make the learning process fun and engaging. *This is where you will have your "own" Bobbie come out or start the video.*

BOBBIE LIVE

Enter eating cake batter or a giant chocolate chip cookie.

- Hello guys, my name is Bobbie, and I am a baker who is hard-working, klutzy, goofy, and maybe slightly messy, but I have a great heart.
- I want to bake the BEST thing that God's heart is craving, and I am willing to do whatever it takes to do it.
- Can I tell you guys a joke?
- Q: Why did the baker choose his job?
- A: Because it's a piece of cake!
- I made this cake one time.

Have Bobbie pull out photo of fancy cake in fancy frame to show. Bobbie gazes lovingly at cake.

- It was *beautiful* and the most *delicious* baked good I had ever tasted.
- Every week I am going to introduce a new secret ingredient so that you can make delicious foods too. I am very excited to see you guys every week!

TICKET TIMER 5 minutes

See Lesson Overview on page 12.

Building anticipation to this moment by celebrating each winner will make these few moments a lot of fun.

Have your container that is holding tickets and timer ready. Have the children pull out their ticket(s). Take one ticket from the container and read the numbers. Continue until time runs out.

ACTIVATION

No Activation this week.

END GAME: FOUR CORNERS 25 minutes

This is a really fun time and something to look forward to at the end of each service. The goal here is fun! Children thrive when fun is just as much a priority as other parts of a lesson.

Explain the rules to the children. Have four preset corners; these could be actual corners in the room, or specific areas in the room that would stand out as four separate areas. Also designate an "out" area; a wall would work perfectly for the "out" area.

To begin the game, have a Caller who is an adult leader or trusted child.

The caller must then close their eyes, coun tdown from ten, and spin in a circle. While this is happening the players select one of the four corners as their own, and go to it. The children must move as quietly as possible so the caller does not know which corner is full of people. Once the caller reaches zero, they call out a corner (1, 2, 3, or 4).

The players in the corresponding corner are then considered out and need to go to the designated out area. The last player standing is the winner and can become the new caller.

NOTE: If there are a lot of players that try to change their corner once the caller has reached zero, you may include the following rule: If you move to a different corner after the caller reaches zero, you are immediately out.

GOODBYE

When children are leaving for the day, take time to connect with the parents and tell them something good that happened with their child during the service.

(See next page for space to write lesson notes.)

LESSON 1 NOTES

Lesson 2
God Is Good

Main Themes

Today we will be learning about the first kingdom core value, God Is Good. We want the children to walk away from this lesson having a better understanding of what God is like, how good He really is, and how much better our lives are with Him in it.

Supply List for Every Lesson

- ☐ Carnival tickets
- ☐ Container (baker's hat) for tickets
- ☐ Folder with Bible memorization charts
- ☐ Blank memorization charts for new kids
- ☐ Stickers for chart completion
- ☐ Two-minute ticket timer
- ☐ Bobbie Baker video and something to the play the video
  Or
- ☐ Live Skit with Bobbie's costume and props

Supply List for Lesson 2

- ☐ Ball or object to throw
- ☐ Soft worship music (best without words)
- ☐ Hula hoops (6-10)
- ☐ Bobbie Baker props (if doing live skit):
  - ☐ Chef hat
  - ☐ Mustache
  - ☐ Apron
  - ☐ Recipe book "Bible"
  - ☐ Giant chocolate bar for Bobbie to eat
  - ☐ Milk chocolate bar
  - ☐ Bitter dark chocolate

CONNECT TIME: SILENT BALL
10 minutes

Have all the players begin by standing in a circle. Whoever is leading will be the only one who can speak. The leader is the only one who can decide who is out. Begin by throwing the ball to any player in the circle. Once the other player catches the ball they may then throw the ball to any other player in the circle. The game continues in this fashion until every player is out.

Ways to get out:
- If a player throws the ball too hard, too high, or too low for the receiving player to catch. The leader decides on whether or not the ball was catchable.
- If a player throws a ball to the receiver and the receiver drops the ball, the receiver is out.
- If any player talks or makes any noise.

BIBLE MEMORIZATION 30 minutes

Matthew 7:7

Ask, and it will be given to you. Search, and you will find. Knock, and the door will be opened to you. (NIRV)

GAME: HAND SIGNALS
30 minutes

Teach the children the verse using hand signals. As you say the verse, have them do the signal and repeat the words after you.

- **"Ask and it will..."**: Put both hands out palms up in front of you like you are receiving a gift.
- **"Be given to you"**: Put both hands on your heart.

GAME: HAND SIGNALS GAME
(Continued)

- **"Search, and you will find":** Make both hands like binoculars and put them over your eyes.
- **"Knock, and the door will be opened to you":** Make a knocking motion with one hand.
- You'll repeat this process with the children about five times. Once the children think they know the verse, they can go to the designated leader to share.
- If they remember the verse, give them the prize, and if they have forgotten, have the child return to the group to practice the verse.
  - This is also the time where they get to put their sticker on their Bible memorization chart.

TEACHING INTRO 5 minutes

- Welcome back to our kingdom core value lesson.
- Today we are learning about the core value, God Is Good.
- God is really good and the more we know about Him, the more we discover how good He is.
- Raise your hand if you can think of the best day you ever had?

Have some of the children share their best day, and comment on how amazing that is!

- God is even better than that best day!

BOBBIE BAKER 5 minutes

Bobbie will help break down the kingdom core value, God Is Good, and make the learning process fun and engaging. *This is where you will have your "own" Bobbie come out or start the video.*

(continued on next page)

BOBBIE BAKER (continued)

BOBBIE LIVE

Enter eating a chocolate bar and having just taken a big bite.

- Hi, if you don't remember me, my name is Bobbie Baker. Can I tell you guys a joke?

- What do you call a sheep covered in chocolate?

- A Candy Baa.

- I like to make tasty food, but I also like to tell people about my secret recipes. In my recipe book (have a Bible recipe book prop) it tells me in Psalm 34 to "Taste and see that the Lord is good...." I decided to try it out and follow the recipe! So today, I made some chocolate for you all to try.

Have a milk chocolate bar and a very high percentage dark chocolate bar.

- I call them Bobbie's Chocolate bars. In one of them I put this goodness ingredient, and the other I left the goodness ingredient out of the recipe.

- I need a volunteer to help me by taste testing them. Who wants to help?

- I want you to taste this one, and I will taste one.

Give the child a bit of the milk chocolate and some of the dark chocolate. Make sure to laugh and have a strong reaction to both items they eat.

- See, just like there was a secret ingredient to make these chocolate bars taste excellent, there is a secret ingredient to our lives, and God has it for you. It's His GOODNESS, and it is so amazing.

- I discovered this secret ingredient a long time ago. When I found out I was having a son, I knew I was going to love him even before I saw him.

- When I met him, I had so much love in me, water started bursting out my eyes... I cried.

- My son didn't have to do anything to earn my love, he just gets it because he's mine. That's how God loves you too. You don't have to earn God's love, because He is a good Father who loves you just because you're His children.

- That's the best news ever isn't it!

- Can't wait to see you next week and share another of my secret recipes with you!

ACTIVATION: SEEING GOD'S GOODNESS
10 minutes

GOAL

To connect the children to God's goodness by having them remember times where He has showed up for them or their families.

> **TEACHER**
>
> **Thank you Bobbie, that was helpful to hear. How many of you have stories of times that God has been really good to you? Can some of you come up to the front and share with the room?**

Have about 3-5 children share during this time.

> **TEACHER**
>
> **Now, I want us to have some time to hang out with God and hear some of the promises He has for us.**

SETUP

- Turn the lights down low, but not off.
- Play some calm worship music (songs that are instrumental and without words are the best). Have all the children find a spot in the room by themselves where they can lay flat on their backs. As soon as the room is set up you can begin.

> **TEACHER**
>
> - **Now, I want you to close your eyes for a minute and picture Jesus. As soon as you see Him with your eyes still closed, give me a thumbs up. Now I am going to read a verse from the Bible over you.**
> - **Jeremiah 29:11 - "'I know the plans I have for you,' announces the Lord. 'I want you to enjoy success. I do not plan to harm you. I will give you hope for the years to come'" (NIRV).**
> - **Now, with your eyes closed, I want you to say to God, "Show me a picture of what your goodness looks like."**
> - **If you want to share, come to the front to tell us what God showed you.**

Have the children share what they experienced for about five minutes. If what the child share feels vague, ask clarifying questions about what they saw and experienced. Affirm their experience!

TICKET TIMER 5 minutes

See Lesson Overview on page 12.

Building anticipation to this moment by celebrating each winner will make these few moments a lot of fun.

Have your container that is holding tickets, a ticket timer ready and have the children pull out their tickets. From the container, take out one ticket at a time, and read it until a winner is identified.

END GAME: LEAPING LILY PADS
25 minutes

This is a really fun time and something to look forward to at the end of each service. The goal here is fun! Children thrive when fun is just as much a priority as other parts of a lesson.

Divide your room into two teams. Spread the hula hoops in a curved line from one wall to another, preferably on the other side of the room.

The two teams that have been evenly divided will be competing against each other to reach the opposing side.

When the game leader says go, one player from each team will begin hopping with feet together from one hula hoop to the next until they meet the opposing player.

When the two players meet, they must play Rock, Paper, Scissors. Have them count to three, and choose rock, paper, or scissors.

The player that wins gets to continue jumping through the hula hoops, while the losing player steps out of the hula hoops, and runs to the back of their team's line. Then the next player on the losing player's team will begin hopping through the hula hoops from the beginning. The new player will then meet the opposing player, and repeat the process of rock, paper, scissors.

This continues until a player finds themselves in the last hula hoop on the opposing team's side and that team wins.

GOODBYE

When children are leaving for the day, take time to connect with the parents and tell them something good that happened with their child during the service.

LESSON 2 NOTES

Lesson 3
Salvation Creates Joyful Identity

Supply List for Every Lesson

- ☐ Carnival tickets
- ☐ Container (baker's hat) for tickets
- ☐ Folder with Bible memorization charts
- ☐ Blank memorization charts for new kids
- ☐ Stickers for chart completion
- ☐ Two-minute ticket timer
- ☐ Bobbie Baker video and something to the play the video
  Or
- ☐ Live Skit with Bobbie's costume and props

Supply List for Lesson 3

- ☐ Coloring pages (found in Appendix)
- ☐ Coloring utensils
- ☐ Papers with the verse phrases written
- ☐ Tape
- ☐ Bobbie Baker props (if doing live skit):
  - ☐ Chef hat
  - ☐ Mustache
  - ☐ Apron
  - ☐ Recipe book "Bible"
  - ☐ Rainbow sprinkles shaker

Main Themes

For this lesson, we will be breaking down the kingdom core value, Salvation Creates Joyful Identity. The children will better understand what salvation means, and the result of salvation is a life full of joy. They will get the opportunity to ask Jesus into their hearts if they have not yet done this.

CONNECT TIME 10 minutes

For this connect time activity the children will be coloring pictures of Bobbie Baker that are provided in the Appendix. Use this coloring time to connect with the children and ask them how their week was. Give them compliments on how they are doing on their coloring.

BIBLE MEMORIZATION 30 minutes

Romans 5:8

But here is how God has shown His love for us. While we were still sinners, Christ died for us. (NIRV)

GAME: SCRAMBLED SCRIPTURE
30 minutes

Ask for six volunteers to come to the front of the room. Have separate sheets of paper with phrases from the verse written on each piece of paper.

- **1st Paper:** Romans 5:8
- **2nd Paper:** But here is how
- **3rd Paper:** God has shown
- **4th Paper:** His love for us
- **5th Paper:** While we were still sinners
- **6th Paper:** Christ died for us

- Tape these papers to the backs of six different kids and have the remaining children try to organize them into the correct order.
- Once the children are in the right order, have the children say it all together several times to learn the verse.

GAME: SCRAMBLED SCRIPTURE
(Continued)

- Play this two or three times with different children so everyone has a chance to learn the verse.
- Once the children think they know the verse, they can go to the designated leader to share. If they remember the verse, give them the prize. If they have forgotten, have the child return to the group to practice the verse.
  - This is also the time where they get to put their sticker on their Bible memorization chart when they have memorized the verse.

TEACHING INTRO 5 minutes

- **Last week we got to experience the goodness of God, and this week we are going to talk about how Salvation Creates Joyful Identity.**
- **That sounds pretty intense, but it's going to be fun. So let's dig in!**
- **Does anyone know what salvation is or what it means?**

Allow time for children to answer.

- **Salvation is Jesus taking what we deserve and giving us what He deserves. Jesus died on the cross, and it saved us from what we deserved.**
- **When we want salvation to be a part of our lives, all we have to do is ask Jesus for it.**
- **How many of you already have Jesus in your heart?**

Allow children to raise hands in answer.

- **Raise your hand if you have ever helped someone accept Jesus into their hearts!**

Allow time for children to raise hands.

BOBBIE BAKER 5 minutes

Bobbie will help break down the kingdom core value and make the learning process fun and engaging. *This is where you will have your "own" Bobbie come out or start the video.*

BOBBIE LIVE

Enter eating and shaking sprinkles into his mouth.

- I heard you guys talking about another secret ingredient! Salvation!!! I have a craaaazy story about when I got saved. But before we talk about that, I have a joke for you.

- Q: What does it do before it rains candy?

- A: It sprinkles!

- So...It was a super sunny day, and I felt super sad. I had run out of my favorite rainbow sprinkles that I put on my favorite giant cookies I make.

- I had never talked to God before this, but I decided to give it a try. I started talking to Him, and it was craaazy; I could hear Him, like I can hear you right now.

- He said, "I love you Bobbie, and I want to save you from all the sadness you feel right now, and all the pain and sadness you feel right now. I want to be your friend, and show you all my love. Just give me your pain and sadness, and I will give you peace, hope, faith, and most importantly LOVE."

- I tried to find where His voice was coming from, but I couldn't. So I said, "YES, I want to be your friend! Will you take my sadness and pain? I want what you have for me."

- Then all of a sudden I felt the best I've ever felt in my entire life! Now, instead of just baking because I like it; I bake because I love Jesus, and He is my source of joy.

- Now that Jesus is in my heart, I feel even more joy than I feel when I see rainbow sprinkles on my giant cookies...which is saying a whole lot.

- See you all next time!

ACTIVATION: INVITATION TO SALVATION
10 minutes

GOAL

Provide a time where the children can start or restart their relationship with Jesus.

TEACHER

- **Thank you Bobbie! Isn't his story amazing? Bobbie has Jesus in his heart now, and he knows who he was always meant to be. He has been filled with joy.**

- **When Jesus died on the cross, He won the ultimate victory and set us free from sin, lies, and sickness. He gave us freedom, truth, health, and joy!**

- **If you do not know Jesus and would like to ask Him into your heart and be friends with Him forever, come up to the front and stand with me.**

- **If you are struggling with sadness, sickness, or anything else and would like Holy Spirit to fill you with joy, and health, come up here, and we will pray with you.**

Spend this time praying with the children who are accepting the invitation. If you hear Holy Spirit leading you to pray or say something specific, share.

TICKET TIMER 5 minutes

See Lesson Overview on page 12.

Building anticipation to this moment by celebrating each winner will make these few moments a lot of fun.

Have your container that is holding tickets, a ticket timer ready and have the children pull out their tickets. From the container, take out one ticket at a time, and continue to read out numbers until the timer runs out.

END GAME: NIGHT AT THE MUSEUM
25 minutes

This is a really fun time and something to look forward to at the end of each service. The goal here is fun! Children thrive when fun is just as much a priority as other parts of a lesson.

Choose a security guard (adult leader or trusted child), and statues (the rest of the children in the room). Assign a designated "out" area (a wall works great).

The security guard closes his/her eyes and counts down from ten, while the statues pose like statues. After the security guard reaches zero, he/she opens his/her eyes and studies the statues.

The statues may move at any time, but if the security guard sees them move (body movement, not breathing or blinking), then they are out. The goal of this game is to be the last standing statue.

If a player is the last statue standing, they become the security guard, and the game begins again with all the players.

During game play, the statues are required to move at least a little bit. If a player does not move for an extended period of time (three to five minutes), then they are given thirty seconds to make a movement, or they are out.

If the last few players are too hard to get out, increase the difficulty by including to include facial movements and blinking.

GOODBYE

When children are leaving for the day, take time to connect with the parents and tell them something good that happened with their child during the service. The children will need their Bibles for the lesson next week, so remind the children and parents about this on their way out.

LESSON 3 NOTES

Lesson 4
Responsive to Grace

Main Themes

For this lesson the children will learn how their attitude should be toward the grace made available to them at the cross as well as the power of choice and self control.

Supply List for Every Lesson

- ☐ Carnival tickets
- ☐ Container (baker's hat) for tickets
- ☐ Folder with Bible memorization charts
- ☐ Blank memorization charts for new kids
- ☐ Stickers for chart completion
- ☐ Two-minute ticket timer
- ☐ Bobbie Baker video and something to the play the video
  Or
- ☐ Live Skit with Bobbie's costume and props

Supply List for Lesson 4

- ☐ Bag filled with "get to know you" questions
- ☐ Red printed or written scripture phrases
- ☐ Blue printed or written scripture phrases
- ☐ Tape
- ☐ Bibles (several for children to use)
- ☐ Bucket with "grace" label on it
- ☐ Slips of paper
- ☐ Pencils/writing utensils
- ☐ Bobbie Baker props (if doing live skit):
  - ☐ Chef hat
  - ☐ Mustache
  - ☐ Apron
  - ☐ Recipe book "Bible"
  - ☐ Eggs (3 hard-boiled or raw)
  - ☐ Cookie

CONNECT TIME 10 minutes

Have a bag filled with silly "get to know you" questions. Count down from ten and pass the bag in a circle. When you get to zero, the person it lands on has to reach their hand in a bag to pull out a question and answer the question.

Note: You will be using this activity again in the lesson so make sure to hang on to it after this activity.

Here are some possible questions to get you started:

- Would you rather have a giant gummy bear that filled this room or a pickle-flavored shoe?
- If you were a talking cat, what color would you be and why?
- If you made your own candy pizza, what toppings would you put on top?
- If you found twenty dollars and could only buy bugs from a pet store with it, what would you name one of the bugs?
- Would you rather giggle every time someone sneezes or have your shoes untie themselves every time you ate a cookie?

- _____

- _____

- _____

If a child has already answered a specific question, feel free to have them choose a different question to answer.

BIBLE MEMORIZATION 30 minutes

Ephesians 2:8-9

God's grace has saved you because of your faith in Christ. Your salvation doesn't come from anything you do. It is God's gift. It is not based on anything you have done. No one can brag about earning it. (NIRV)

GAME: SCRIPTURE RACE
30 Minutes

- Break your children into two even teams: red team and blue team.

- Have this week's Bible memorization verse written out on a few pieces of paper, separated and hung around the room you are in, taped to the walls.

- Write out or print the separated verse pages on two different color pages, one for red team and one for blue.

- When you say go, the children need to find all the pieces of paper for their team's color, and use Bibles to find the verse and put their pieces in the correct order.

- Whoever does this first wins! Then have the children memorize the verse.

- Once the children think they know the verse, they can go to the designated leader to share.

- If they remember the verse, give them the prize, and if they have forgotten, have the child return to the group to practice the verse.

  - This is also the time where they get to put their sticker on their Bible memorization chart when they have memorized the verse.

TEACHING INTRO 5 minutes

- If you are ready to hear about our next kingdom core value, throw two hands in the air and yell, "WAHOOOOO!"

- This week we are learning about the core value, Responsive to Grace. We want you to learn what grace means and how we should we live because we have it.

- Grace means that as Christians we are not controlled by God, but we get to choose to follow God. He has an incredible amount of love for us that we don't deserve.

- When Jesus died, He paid for every bad thing we have done and will do. Because of this, we get to choose every day to respond to God's perfect grace and be powerful, responsible, and people with this kind of trust.

TEACHING INTRO (continued)

- Remember, He loves us right where we are, but He loves us too much to leave us in a life that is not His best for us.

- He helps us grow up to be powerful and pure people.

- How many of you want to live that kind of life?

Have children raise their hand to respond.

- I wonder if Bobbie has anything else to say about this? Bobbie?

BOBBIE BAKER 5 minutes

Bobbie will help break down the kingdom core value and make the learning process fun and engaging. *This is where you will have your "own" Bobbie come out or start the video.*

BOBBIE LIVE

Enter from the left of the screen eating a cookie and looking surprised that the children are all in his kitchen.

- Hi everyone, I have missed you all!! Who is ready for a joke?

- Q: What happens when you make an egg laugh?

- A: It cracks up.

- Oh my goodness, gracious!

- I made a BIG mistake the other day.

- I was baking my famous Cheesy Pita Chip pie, and I was using the recipe, but somehow, someway, some distraction happened. I missed putting the eggs in it. The pie was a mess without the eggs, it tasted very terrible. That means really bad.

- Anyways, the eggs are a lot like God's grace.

- You see, in God's recipe book, it tells us that grace is a very important ingredient.

- It is a very strong ingredient. Just like the outside of an egg is strong, but you have to be careful with it as well.

BOBBIE BAKER (continued)

- **You don't get to throw it around like you could other ingredients.**
- **Watch what happens when I juggle these eggs.**

Have Bobbie juggle the eggs and allow a few to fall in sight of the children and break.

- **See, they crack when I use them in the wrong way. I like grace because when we take care of it, we get to receive what Jesus deserved instead of getting what we deserve.**
- **It makes us stronger.**
- **See you all next time!**

ACTIVATION: GRACE COVERING SIN
10 minutes

GOAL
Help the children see how grace redeems anything that was out of alignment in their lives.

SUPPLIES
You will need grace written on a piece of paper and attached to a bucket.

TEACHER

- **The Bible says: Romans 3:23-24 (NIRV) - "Everyone has sinned. No one measures up to God's glory. The free gift of God's grace makes us right with him. Christ Jesus paid the price to set us free."**
- **This means that when we sin, we can be made whole again by Jesus, covering us in grace. All we have to do is come to Him.**
- **How many of you can think of any area right now you would like Jesus to cover in His grace?**
- **I am going to give you a strip of paper, and I want you to write down anything you would like Jesus to cover. Then we are going to throw it in the "grace bucket" in the middle of the room.**

ACTIVATION: GRACE COVERING SIN (continued)

Have the children write down areas that they need grace in. Have a bucket in the middle of the room thats says GRACE, and have the children throw their notes into it.

End by praying over the children in the room that this will feel like a new beginning for them in every area they needed grace, and that those areas will not be areas of struggle again for them.

Have children share with the room what they experienced during this time.

TICKET TIMER 5 minutes

See Lesson Overview on page 12.

Building anticipation to this moment by celebrating each winner will make these few moments a lot of fun.

Have your container that is holding tickets, a ticket timer ready and have the children pull out their tickets. From the container, take out one ticket at a time, and continue to read out numbers until the timer runs out.

END GAME: FOUR CORNERS 25 minutes

This is a really fun time and something to look forward to at the end of each service. The goal here is fun! Children thrive when fun is just as much a priority as other parts of a lesson.

Explain the rules to the children. Have four preset corners; these could be actual corners in the room, or specific areas in the room that would stand out as four separate areas. Also designate an "out" area; a wall would work perfectly for the "out" area.

The caller must then close their eyes, count down from ten, and spin in a circle. While this is happening the players select one of the four corners as their own, and go to it. The children must move as quietly as possible so the caller does not know which corner is full of people. Once the caller reaches zero, they call out a corner (1, 2, 3, or 4).

The players in the corresponding corner, are then considered out and need to go to the designated out area. The last player standing is the winner and can become the new caller.

NOTE: If there are a lot of players that try to change their corner once the caller has reached zero, you may include the following rule: If you move to a different corner after the caller reaches zero, you are immediately out.

GOODBYE

When children are leaving for the day, take time to connect with the parents and tell them something good that happened with their child during the service. Let your children know that they will need to bring a Bible to service next week.

(See next page for space to write lesson notes)

LESSON 4 NOTES

Lesson 5
Focused on His Presence

Main Themes

For this lesson the children will walk away with a greater self awareness of God's presence in their everyday life, and the benefit of always being connected to Holy Spirit.

Supply List for Every Lesson

- ☐ Carnival tickets
- ☐ Container (baker's hat) for tickets
- ☐ Folder with Bible memorization charts
- ☐ Blank memorization charts for new kids
- ☐ Stickers for chart completion
- ☐ Two-minute ticket timer
- ☐ Bobbie Baker video and something to the play the video
  Or
- ☐ Live Skit with Bobbie's costume and props

Supply List for Lesson 5

- ☐ Paper for paper airplanes
- ☐ Markers to color the airplanes
- ☐ Bibles (one for each child)
- ☐ Bobbie Baker props (if doing live skit):
  - ☐ Chef hat
  - ☐ Mustache
  - ☐ Apron
  - ☐ Recipe book "Bible"
  - ☐ Honey

CONNECT TIME: PAPER AIRPLANE COMPETITION 10 minutes

Have children make paper airplanes during this time, and provide markers for them to decorate them. Explain that they cannot throw them until the competition, or they will be disqualified.

At the end of connect time, have all those who would like to participate in the competition take their planes and stand on one side of the room. When you say go, have them throw their airplanes at one time. Whoever's plane goes the farthest will win!

BIBLE MEMORIZATION 30 minutes

John 4:23

But a new time is coming. In fact, it is already here. True worshipers will worship the Father in the Spirit and in truth. They are the kind of worshipers the Father is looking for. (NIRV)

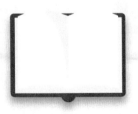

GAME: GETTING TO KNOW THE BIBLE 30 Minutes

This week have the children memorize scripture by simply using a Bible and looking up the verse and learning it. Children may need extra help learning to find the book of John in the Bible. Take some time to explain how to find it, and how to use the index of the Bible.

Once the children think they know the verse, they can go to the designated leader to share. If they remember the verse, give them the prize, and if they have forgotten, have the child return to the group to practice the verse.

This is also the time where they get to put their sticker on their Bible memorization chart when they have memorized the verse.

TEACHING INTRO 5 minutes

- Hey everyone, today we are going to learn about the kingdom core value, Focused on His Presence! Get ready because when you focus on God's presence, you can't help but be changed!

BOBBIE BAKER 5 minutes

Bobbie will help break down the kingdom core value and make the learning process fun and engaging. *This is where you will have your "own" Bobbie come out or start the video.*

BOBBIE LIVE

Bobbie will enter eating a handful of honey.

- Hey everyone, what are you learning about today?
- What!!!! Focused on His presence. I love God's presence and do you guys know His presence tastes so good?
- Ready for my joke?
- Q: Why did the bee get married?
- A: Because he found his honey.
- Yes! His presence is sweet like the honey that I have, and I was just baking with.
- This honey is sticky and it is hard to get off just like God's presence.

Put honey on both hands and stick hands together

- Oh no! My hands are stuck!
- Let me read you this verse from my recipe book while I try and get my hands unstuck. Psalm 34:8 "Taste and see that the Lord is good. Blessed is the person who goes to him for safety."
- If you spend time in God's presence every day, you will see that life is so much more sweet and satisfying.
- Do you guys want to learn how to say goodbye in French? Au revoir! (Oh reh-vah).
- Say it with me! Au revoir. (Oh reh-vah)
- See you all next time!

ACTIVATION: BUILDING AWARENESS OF THE HOLY SPIRIT 5 minutes

GOAL
Help children understand how accessible the Holy Spirit is and how He is everywhere.

TEACHER

- **What do you guys think it means to be "focused on His presence?"** Allow children to answer.
  - **To be focused on His presence is to stay connected to God and partner with what God is doing in every moment.**
  - **It could look like spending time with friends, watching a movie, doing laundry, giving a compliment to the cashier, helping someone carry some groceries, or talking to a friend and being there for them during a hard time.**
  - **It could also be praying for someone or writing a kind note to a stranger. It doesn't matter what we do, just as long as we do it with God.**
- **Any moment you can ask God what He is doing! Do you know the Holy Spirit is everywhere? Well He is.**
- **Let's take a moment to focus on His presence.**
- **Everyone, close our eyes and put our hands on our hearts.**
- **I want you all to say, "Holy Spirit where are you right now in this room?"**
- **Now, I want you all to keep your eyes closed, and point to where the Holy Spirit is in the room right now.**
- **Now I want you to ask, "Holy Spirit what is one thing you want me to know today?**
- **Raise your hand if you heard Holy Spirit say something or you feel Holy Spirit.**
- **I want you raise your hand if you want to share with everyone what Holy Spirit said to you.** Allow children to share with the room.
- **When we keep our focus on His presence, it changes everything!**
- **Try doing this exercise more this week, and tell me next week what happened!**

TICKET TIMER 5 minutes

See Lesson Overview on page 12.

Building anticipation to this moment by celebrating each winner will make these few moments a lot of fun.

Have your container that is holding tickets and timer ready. Have the children pull out their tickets. From the container, take out and read one ticket at a time.

END GAME: MR. FOX 25 minutes

This is a really fun time and something to look forward to at the end of each service. The goal here is fun! Children thrive when fun is just as much a priority as other parts of a lesson.

Choose one child to be Mr. Fox. Have all of the other players line up on the other side of the room you are playing in. Have Mr. Fox face away from the other children playing so they cannot single out specific players to get them out.

- Together, all the players call out, "What time is it, Mr. Fox?"

  - Mr. Fox responds by saying a time that is on the clock.
    Example: 1 o'clock - 12 o'clock.

  - The group then takes that many steps:

    - 1 o'clock would be one step

    - 2 o'clock would be two steps, etc.

- When, the caller playing Mr. Fox is ready, he/she can call out, "dinner time."

  - At this point Mr. Fox turns around and will chase the players to tag as many as possible.

  - If tagged, the players will have go sit in Mr. Fox's pot. To avoid being tagged, players must touch the wall of the starting place.

- On the next turn, players must avoid being tagged by Mr. Fox, and tag their friends out of the pot when they are close enough.

- Play until there is only one player left. This player can become Mr. Fox for the next round.

END GAME: MR. FOX (Xtreme Adaptation)

- Have children close their eyes while Mr. Fox hides somewhere in the room.

- Have another leader be the one that is calling out what time it is.

- When the leader calls out dinner time Mr. Fox will come out of hiding and chase the children back to the starting place.

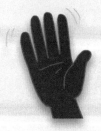

GOODBYE

When children are leaving for the day, take time to connect with the parents and tell them something good that happened with their child during the service.

LESSON 5 NOTES

Lesson 6
Creating Healthy Family

Main Themes

In this lesson, children will learn to see the members of their family through God's eyes, how to honor their family members, and how to love, even when it's difficult.

Supply List for Every Lesson

- ☐ Carnival tickets
- ☐ Container (bakers's hat) for tickets
- ☐ Folder with Bible memorization charts
- ☐ Blank memorization charts for new kids
- ☐ Stickers for chart completion
- ☐ Two-minute ticket timer
- ☐ Bobbie Baker video and something to the play the video

  Or

- ☐ Live Skit with Bobbie's costume and props

Supply List for Lesson 6

- ☐ Ball or object to throw
- ☐ Verse written big on paper or whiteboard
- ☐ Ball or object to pass as "hot potato"
- ☐ Cups of popcorn for all children to eat
- ☐ Napkins
- ☐ Printed family crest paper
- ☐ Coloring utensils
- ☐ Soft worship music
- ☐ Example of family crest paper completed
- ☐ Videos of fainting goats to share with children
- ☐ Bobbie Baker props (if doing live skit):
    - ☐ Chef hat
    - ☐ Mustache
    - ☐ Apron
    - ☐ Recipe book "Bible"
    - ☐ Stick of butter or empty box of butter
    - ☐ Buttered popcorn

CONNECT TIME: SILENT BALL
10 minutes

Have all the players begin by standing in a circle. Whoever is leading will be the only one who can speak. The leader is the only one who can decide who is out. Begin by throwing the ball to any player in the circle. Once the other player catches the ball, they may then throw the ball to any other player in the circle. The game continues in this fashion until every player is out.

Ways to get out:
- If a player throws the ball too hard, too high, or too low for the receiving player to catch. The leader decides on whether or not the ball was catchable.
- If a player throws a ball to the receiver and the receiver drops the ball, the receiver is out.
- If any player talks or makes any noise.

BIBLE MEMORIZATION 30 minutes

Ephesians 1:5

So he decided long ago to adopt us. He adopted us as his children with all the rights children have. He did it because of what Jesus Christ has done. It pleased God to do it. (NIRV)

GAME: HOT POTATO
30 Minutes

- Have the verse written on a piece of paper and tape that paper up on the wall where the children can see it.
- Have all of the children sitting in a circle on the floor where they will be able to see the verse .

GAME: HOT POTATO
(continued)

- Pass the ball around in a circle and count down from ten.

  - Whoever is holding the ball when the time runs out will read the whole verse out loud from the paper.

  - Then all the children will repeat the verse right after. Start the game again and repeat the process until it feels like the children can recite the verse without looking at it.

- Once the children think they know the verse, they can go to the designated leader to share.

- If they remember the verse, give them the prize, and if they have forgotten, have the child return to the group to practice the verse.

  - This is also the time where they get to put their sticker on their Bible memorization chart when they have memorized the verse.

TEACHING INTRO 5 minutes

- Hey guys! Can anyone tell me a story from this last week where you took some time to focus on God's presence and what happened when you did that?

Allow children to share and affirm.

- Today we're learning about the kingdom core value: Creating Healthy Families.

- How many of you have so much fun with your family? How many of you have had hard times, good times, sad times and fun times with your families?

- Did you know that we are also part of a church family called the body of Christ.

- We all have families in Christ, all the people we are with today. When we learn to love them, honor them, and stay connected to them, especially through hard times, we can be even more powerful together.

- This allows us to see God move all over the world!! Now we are going to have some family time for a little bit!

- So we are going to hand out some popcorn to eat while we listen to Bobbie Baker!

BOBBIE BAKER 5 minutes

Bobbie will help break down the kingdom core value and make the learning process fun and engaging. *This is where you will have your "own" Bobbie come out or start the video.*

BOBBIE LIVE

Enter eating buttered popcorn in a messy fashion.

- **Welcome back to my kitchen!**

- **Q: Why did the child throw the butter out the window?**

- **A: To see the butter fly!**

- **Haha! Can someone tell me what you are learning about today?**

Allow children to answer

- **Family! I love family. Is it easy to be in a family?**

Allow children to answer.

- **For me, it is not always easy.**

- **Sometimes I compare myself to my oldest brother who is a much better baker than I am, and that can make me feel less special.**

- **Sometimes I have disagreements with him which are no fun. I have to do my best to choose love for my brothers and sisters in my family.**

- **Do you know we cannot have love without choice because without choice, we cannot really have love.**

- **If you were forced to feel love, love would not feel good or be worth as much.**

- **So with this, we get to choose to honor our families, and we get to choose to love our families.**

- **Being part of a family is like this butter because when you do family really well, it adds flavor to every area of your life.**

- **Hope you guys have the best time learning more about this. Good-bye for today!**

ACTIVATION: FAMILY CREST
10 minutes

GOAL

Have a time of thinking and partnering with God to focus on the best parts of their families.

TEACHER

- **Does anyone know what a family crest is?**

Allow children to answer.

- **A family crest was an old way to learn about a family, their history and what they stood for just by looking at an image that had different pictures and symbols on it.**

Show completed family crest.

- **This is my family crest.**

Show what you drew and explain why you added the elements you did.

- **Right now we want to dream with God about what is possible for our families, and the ways He wants our families to look even healthier.**

If you are able to, dim the lights and play some worship music to set the tone of the moment.

- **I want everyone to close your eyes and picture yourself sitting somewhere super comfy. It might be a couch or a huge bean bag or somewhere like this.**

- **Now, I want you to imagine Jesus walking into the room and sitting down with you.**

- **Imagine that Jesus has a photo album of your whole family.**

  - **Raise your hand if you can see it!**

- **Now with your eyes closed, I want you to imagine Him showing you pictures of your family, and I want you to ask Him a question.**

  - **I want you to ask Jesus what His purpose for your family is?**

  - **Ask Him what good things He wants to bring to your family?**

  - **Now ask Him what good things your family can bring to the people around you?**

(contiued on next page)

ACTIVATION: FAMILY CREST
(continued)

- **Now I want everyone to open your eyes.**

Hand out a family crest to each child.

- **I want you to draw on your family crest what Jesus showed you**

Find the blank family crest in the Appendix.

- **When you go home, you can share it with your family, and tell them what the Holy Spirit shared with you.**

NOTE

If you have time at the end of this lesson, have a few children share about their family crest, and what it means to them.

TICKET TIMER 5 minutes

See Lesson Overview on page 12.

Building anticipation to this moment by celebrating each winner will make these few moments a lot of fun.

Have your container that is holding tickets, a ticket timer ready and have the children pull out their tickets. From the container, take out one ticket at a time, and continue to read out numbers until the timer runs out.

END GAME: FAINTING GOATS
25 minutes

This is a really fun time and something to look forward to at the end of each service. The goal here is fun! Children thrive when fun is just as much a priority as other parts of a lesson.

Before playing this game, look up some videos online of fainting goats to show your children. Children cannot run in this game but have to speed walk. Speed walking means that one foot has to be on the ground at a time otherwise it is running.

END GAME: FAINTING GOATS
(continued)

One person is chosen as the shepherd. Whoever the shepherd touches becomes the new shepherd.

The goats can fall to the ground to avoid being tagged for up to ten seconds. As long as they are on the ground, they are safe. The goat can't fall to the ground unless the shepherd is ten feet away or closer.

NOTE: This game is very tiring.

GOODBYE

When children are leaving for the day, take time to connect with the parents and tell them something good that happened with their child during the service. Let parents know that their child will need to bring their Bible for next week's lesson.

LESSON 6 NOTES

LESSON 6 NOTES

Lesson 7
God's Word Transforms

Main Themes

In this lesson, kids will gain a passion for God's Word, and learn to interract with Scripture by listening to the Holy Spirit.

Supply List for Every Lesson

- ☐ Carnival tickets
- ☐ Container (baker's hat) for tickets
- ☐ Folder with Bible memorization charts
- ☐ Blank memorization charts for new kids
- ☐ Stickers for chart completion
- ☐ Two-minute ticket timer
- ☐ Bobbie Baker video and something to the play the video
  - **Or**
- ☐ Live Skit with Bobbie's costume and props

Supply List for Lesson 7

- ☐ Ball to throw
- ☐ Verse phrases on paper taped to the floor for hopscotch
- ☐ Bobbie Baker props (if doing live skit):
  - ☐ Chef hat
  - ☐ Mustache
  - ☐ Apron
  - ☐ Recipe book "Bible"
  - ☐ Big French baguette for Bobbie to eat
  - ☐ Bread with yeast (fluffy)
  - ☐ Bread without yeast (compact and dry for dramatic effect)
  - ☐ Yeast

CONNECT TIME 10 minutes

Have children learn more about each other by standing in a circle and throwing a ball (or object) to each other across the circle. When children catch it, they either have to tell one fact about themselves or name a pizza topping. When children run out of normal toppings, they can start naming ridiculous things that they can think of that would be funny on a pizza, for example: gummy bears, dog food, or pop rocks.

BIBLE MEMORIZATION 30 minutes

Psalm 119:11

I have hidden your word in my heart so that I won't sin against you. (NIRV)

GAME: SCRIPTURE HOPSCOTCH
30 Minutes

Say the scripture verse four or five times with the children out loud so they get familiar with the verse. Write out the words to the verse on paper, and have the children line up and try to say the verse while hopscotching. They will jump on the single squares with one foot and double squares with two feet. Encourage them to go slowly at first!

Write out the verse and place papers out like the diagram to the right.

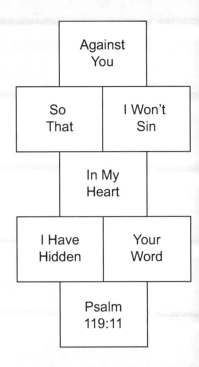

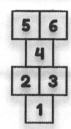

GAME: SCRIPTURE HOPSCOTCH
(continued)

- Once the children think they know the verse, they can go to the designated leader to share.

- If they remember the verse, give them the prize, and if they have forgotten, have the child return to the group to practice the verse.

  - This is also the time where they get to put their sticker on their Bible memorization chart when they have memorized the verse.

TEACHING INTRO 5 minutes

- **Welcome to another day of learning about kingdom core values.**

- **How many of you remembered to bring your Bible to church today?**

- **Oh good! Well today we are going to talk about the core value, God's Word Transforms.**

- **Why do you think scripture is important?**

Allow children to answer.

- **Why do we need it?**

Allow children to answer.

- **Those are some good answers.**

- **As Christians we believe that God speaks through scripture as much as He speaks to us during our daily lives.**

- **We get to know God more by reading the Bible and understanding what scripture says.**

- **How many of you get to know your friends by sitting in two different rooms and not talking to each other?**

Allow children to answer.

- **It's impossible to get to know a friend by being in two different places and not actually talking to them.**

- It's the same way with God, in order to get to know Him more, we have to spend time with Him and talk!

- There's many ways for God to talk to us, and one of those ways are through His Word, the Bible.

- This is what the Bible has to say about this:

  - James 1:23-25 (ICB)
    A person who hears God's teaching and does nothing is like a man looking in a mirror. He sees his face, then goes away and quickly forgets what he looked like. But the truly happy person is the one who carefully studies God's perfect law that makes people free. He continues to study it. He listens to God's teaching and does not forget what he heard. Then he obeys what God's teaching says. When he does this, it makes him happy.

- Who can tell me some ways you read the Bible at home?

Allow children to answer.

- Now, let me tell you my favorite way to read the Bible. Share how you like to read the Bible.

- Now, who is ready to welcome Bobbie?! I am sure he has a lot more to say about this subject. Let's chant his name for him to come out. "Bobbie! Bobbie! Bobbie! Bobbie!"

BOBBIE BAKER 5 minutes

Bobbie will help break down the kingdom core value and make the learning process fun and engaging. *This is where you will have your "own" Bobbie come out or start the video.*

BOBBIE LIVE

Bobbie will enter eating a giant piece of French bread

- **Hello everyone! How are you all.**

Pause to allow children to answer.

- **What are you guys talking about today?**

Pause to allow children to answer

- **God's Word Transforms!**

- **Oh wow!**

- **I love that because God's Word has transformed so much of my life.**

- **If I did not have God's Word, you wouldn't even recognize me!**

- **Let me show you what I mean!**

- **God's Word is like this yeast** (pull out yeast). **Yeast is a special ingredient that helps bread become bread.**

- **When you have yeast, your bread looks like this** (show them the bread). **It is fluffy, and delicious. The way it was meant to be.**

- **When it does not have the yeast, the bread looks like this** (show them yeastless bread). **It is hard and does not taste good.**

- **Can I have a child come up and touch both breads and tell us which one feels right?**

Invite child up and interact with him or her.

- **When we have God's Word in our life, it transforms us like it does this bread.**

- **We become the people we are meant to be because we know who we are in God!**

- **In Matthew 4:4 (NIV) it says, "Jesus answered, 'It is written: "Man shall not live on bread alone, but on every word that comes from the mouth of God."'"**

- **Oh, I almost forgot! I have a joke for you.**

- **Q: When does bread rise?**

- **A: When you yeast expect it to.**

- **See you next time!**

ACTIVATION: HUNGER FOR THE WORD
10 minutes

GOAL

Have the children receive an impartation of a hunger and passion for God's Word from the Holy Spirit.

TEACHER

- Now I want to pray for all of you to have a hunger for the Bible in your life. Everyone, put your hands on your stomach and say, "Holy Spirit give me a hunger for the Bible and for your Word."

- Raise your hand if you felt something when we prayed?

- Yeah! That is the Holy Spirit moving in you. His favorite book is the Bible, and He loves it when you read it and love it too!

- Now, I want you all to find a quiet spot in the room and open your Bible. Read some scripture for about three minutes while we put on some worship music.

Play some worship music you think your children would enjoy.

- You can read from any book you like. If you don't know where to start, you can read from the first book and first chapter of the Bible, Genesis 1.

- This is a really great story about God making the whole world.

Allow the children to read for a while and wrap up this time by having the children share what they read and what it meant to them.

TICKET TIMER 5 minutes

See Lesson Overview on page 12.

Building anticipation to this moment by celebrating each winner will make these few moments a lot of fun.

Have your container that is holding tickets and timer ready. Have the children pull out their tickets. From the container, take out and read one ticket at a time.

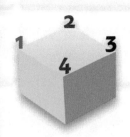

END GAME: FOUR CORNERS 25 minutes

This is a really fun time and something to look forward to at the end of each service. The goal here is fun! Children thrive when fun is just as much a priority as other parts of a lesson.

Explain the rules to the children. Have four preset corners; these could be actual corners in the room, or specific areas in the room that would stand out as four separate areas. Also designate an "out" area; a wall would work perfectly for the out area.

To begin the game, have a Caller who is an adult leader or trusted child.

The caller must then close their eyes, count down from ten, and spin in a circle. While this is happening the players select one of the four corners as their own, and go to it. The children must move as quietly as possible so the caller does not know which corner is full of people. Once the caller reaches zero, they call out a corner (1, 2, 3, or 4).

The players in the corresponding corner are then considered out and need to go to the designated out area. The last player standing is the winner and can become the new caller.

NOTE: If there are a lot of players that try to change their corner once the caller has reached zero, you may include the following rule: If you move to a different corner after the caller reaches zero, you are immediately out.

GOODBYE

When children are leaving for the day, take time to connect with the parents and tell them something good that happened with their child during the service. Let parents know that their child will need to bring their Bible for next week's lesson.

(See next page for space to write lesson notes)

LESSON 7 NOTES

Lesson 8
God Is Still Speaking

Main Themes

For this lesson will learn God speaks to us today. They are able to hear God's voice for other people.

Supply List for Every Lesson

- ☐ Carnival tickets
- ☐ Container (baker's hat) for tickets
- ☐ Folder with Bible memorization charts
- ☐ Blank memorization charts for new kids
- ☐ Stickers for chart completion
- ☐ Two-minute ticket timer
- ☐ Bobbie Baker video and something to the play the video
  Or
- ☐ Live Skit with Bobbie's costume and props

Supply List for Lesson 8

- ☐ Ball to throw
- ☐ Bibles (for children)
- ☐ Markers
- ☐ Blank paper on wall
- ☐ Tape
- ☐ Blank paper for children
- ☐ Coloring utensils
- ☐ Hula hoops (6-10)
- ☐ Bobbie Baker props (if doing live skit):
  - ☐ Chef hat
  - ☐ Mustache
  - ☐ Apron
  - ☐ Recipe book "Bible"
  - ☐ Bottle of olive oil
  - ☐ Wedge of cheese

CONNECT TIME: SILENT BALL
10 minutes

Have all the players begin by standing in a circle. Whoever is leading will be the only one who can speak. The leader is the only one who can decide who is out. Begin by throwing the ball to any player in the circle. Once the other player catches the ball they may then throw the ball to any other player in the circle. The game continues in this fashion until every player is out.

Ways to get out:

- If a player throws the ball too hard, too high, or too low for the receiving player to catch. The leader decides on whether or not the ball was catchable.
- If a player throws a ball to the receiver and the receiver drops the ball, the receiver is out.
- If any player talks or makes any noise.

BIBLE MEMORIZATION 30 minutes

1 Corinthians 14:3

But the person who prophesies speaks to people. That person prophecies to make people stronger, to give them hope, and to comfort them. (NIRV)

GAME: BIBLE VERSE RELAY RACE
30 minutes

This game will be played relay style, one child at a time. The children will run across the room and write down all the words until the verse is completely written out on paper. There are a total of twenty-three words, so if you have less children than this in your room, some children will go more than once.

GAME: BIBLE VERSE RELAY RACE
(Continued)

- To set up this game, have Bibles out or have the children grab their personal Bibles. Then tell the children the scripture reference and have them find it in the Bible.
- Tape a 9x11 piece of blank paper on the opposite side of the room and have the children read the scripture from the Bible.
- The children will memorize the verse, one word at a time, run to the paper and write down the verse.
- Once the verse is finished, have the children bring the paper back to the mat and have everyone learn the whole verse by saying it together.
- Once the children think they know the verse, they can go to the designated leader to share.
- If they remember the verse, give them the prize, and if they have forgotten, have the child return to the group to practice the verse.
    - This is also the time where they get to put their sticker on their Bible memorization chart.

TEACHING INTRO 5 minutes

- **Hey guys, today we are talking about the kingdom core value, God Is Still Speaking.**

- **Who can tell me one way we can hear God's voice?**

Allow the children to answer.

    - **Yes! Prophecy.**

- **Can someone come up and tell me the verse you memorized today?**

Allow a child to say the verse they memorized.

- **Yes, it was 1 Corinthians 14:3. The one who prophesies speaks to people for their strengthening, encouraging and comfort.**

- **When God speaks to us and through us, we know it is God because it makes people feel stronger, happier and closer to Him.**

- **Also, God is regularly speaking, and all we have to do is listen for His voice and read His words. Then we will be changed from the inside out.**

TEACHING INTRO (continued)

- Today we are going to learn how to hear God's voice for other people, and it is going to be super fun!
- Now who is ready to see Bobbie?
- Bobbie, come on out!!

BOBBIE BAKER 5 minutes

Bobbie will help break down the kingdom core value and make the learning process fun and engaging. *This is where you will have your "own" Bobbie come out or start the video.*

BOBBIE LIVE

Bobbie will enter eating a wedge of cheese.

- Hey everyone, I have missed you.
- How many of you think this cheese I am eating looks delicious.

Allow the children to answer.

- Well, it reminds me of a joke.
- Ready for a joke?
- Q: What animal needs oil?
- A: A mouse because it squeaks.
- What are you guys talking about today for the lesson?
- Aww, you don't know?
- Let me remind you: you are talking about God, and how He is still speaking.
- There are a lot of people in the church today that don't believe God can still talk.
- I know, hard to believe right???
- I actually did not know that God could speak until my friend, who's a gold miner, taught me how to look for the gold in people and their hearts.
- God speaking is as real as this olive oil I am holding. Hold up the olive oil.

BOBBIE BAKER (continued)

- How do you know if it is God speaking to you?
  - Well, when you hear His voice, it is like this oil. Good tasting and healthy for your heart.
- Words from God are good tasting because they usually are kinder and smarter than your own ideas.
- They are full of hope and consistent with what He has said in the Bible.
- When you hear His voice, you should feel God's Father-heart toward you and others.
- Now I am going to prophesy over one of you! Who wants a word?

Pick a child from the group and give them a prophetic word.

- How did that make you feel?

Have the child who received the prophetic word share.

- Oh good! That is what happens when you give someone a prophetic word from God. It makes you feel amazing!
- Now, you guys are going to do this too. See you next time!

ACTIVATION: HEARING GOD 10 minutes

GOAL

Demonstrate to the children that hearing God is easy, and it is an amazing way to show others the love of Father God.

TEACHER

- How many of you have ever had a hard time hearing God?

Have about 3-5 children share during this time.

- Well, we have a simple tool to help you listen to God. Get comfortable on the floor and close your eyes.
  - Picture a blank whiteboard, like the one you would see in a classroom.
  - Now, say this with me, "Jesus, would you please draw a

ACTIVATION: HEARING GOD (continued)

picture on the whiteboard?"
- Now watch to see what He draws.
- When He's done, open your eyes and draw what He drew on your whiteboard on the piece of paper in front of you.
- Now I want you to close your eyes again and say, "Jesus, please tell me what it means?" Write that down too.
- Now you have a prophetic word! Great job.
- Who would like to come up to the front and show the room what God showed you?

Have about 3-5 children share during this time.

- Sometimes what God tells us is just for us, so it is okay if you do not want to share.

TICKET TIMER 5 minutes

See Lesson Overview on page 12.

Building anticipation to this moment by celebrating each winner will make these few moments a lot of fun.

Have your container that is holding tickets, a ticket timer ready and have the children pull out their tickets. From the container, take out one ticket at a time, and read it until a winner is identified.

END GAME: LEAPING LILY PADS
25 minutes

This is a really fun time and something to look forward to at the end of each service. The goal here is fun! Children thrive when fun is just as much a priority as other parts of a lesson.

END GAME: LEAPING LILY PADS
(continued)

Divide your room into two teams. Spread the hula hoops in a curved line from one wall to another, preferably on the other side of the room.

The two teams that have been evenly divided will be competing against each other to reach the opposing side.

When the game leader says go, one player from each team will begin hopping with feet together from one hula hoop to the next until they meet the opposing player.

When the two players meet, they must play Rock, Paper, Scissors. Have them count to three, and choose rock, paper, or scissors.

The player that wins gets to continue jumping through the hula hoops, while the losing player steps out of the hula hoops, and runs to the back of their team's line. Then the next player on the losing player's team will begin hopping through the hula hoops from the beginning. The new player will then meet the opposing player, and repeat the process of rock, paper, scissors.

This continues until a player finds themselves in the last hula hoop on the opposing team's side and that team wins.

GOODBYE

When children are leaving for the day, take time to connect with the parents and tell them something good that happened with their child during the service.

(See next page for space to write lesson notes)

LESSON 8 NOTES

Lesson 9
Jesus Empowers Supernatural Ministry

Supply List for Every Lesson

- ☐ Carnival tickets
- ☐ Container (baker's hat) for tickets
- ☐ Folder with Bible memorization charts
- ☐ Blank memorization charts for new kids
- ☐ Stickers for chart completion
- ☐ Two-minute ticket timer
- ☐ Bobbie Baker video and something to the play the video
  Or
- ☐ Live Skit with Bobbie's costume and props

Supply List for Lesson 9

- ☐ Coloring pages (found in Appendix)
- ☐ Coloring utensils
- ☐ Paper with verse printed (enough for every child)
- ☐ Dice
- ☐ Bobbie Baker props (if doing live skit):
  - ☐ Chef hat
  - ☐ Mustache
  - ☐ Apron
  - ☐ Recipe book "Bible"
  - ☐ Jar of sugar
  - ☐ Large rainbow lollipop

Main Themes

The lesson today is that Jesus empowers supernatural ministry. Today's mission is to take everything the children have learned so far and teach them how to reach people who do not know Jesus personally!

CONNECT TIME 10 minutes

For this connect time activity the children will be coloring pictures of Bobbie Baker that are provided in the Appendix. Use this coloring time to connect with the children and ask them how their week was. Give them compliments on how they are doing on their coloring.

BIBLE MEMORIZATION 30 minutes

1 Thessalonians 1:5

Our good news didn't come to you only in words. It came with power. It came with the Holy Spirit's help. He gave us complete faith in what we were preaching. You know how we lived among you for your good. (NIRV)

GAME: DRAWING THE VERSE
30 minutes

TEACHER
- Hand out the Drawing-the-Verse activity page found in the Appendix.
- The children will use their Bibles to look up 1 Thessalonians 1:5 in their Bible. Have them write the verse out on their activity sheets, and then have the children draw a picture of what the verse means to them.
- Once they have completed the activity sheet, the children will read the verse they have written out to continue memorizing the verse.
- Once the children think they know the verse, they can go to the designated leader to share. If they remember the verse, give them the prize, and if they have forgotten, have the child return to the group to practice the verse.
  - This is also the time where they get to put their sticker on their Bible memorization chart when they have memorized the verse.

TEACHING INTRO 5 minutes

- Today, we are learning about the kingdom core value that Jesus empowers supernatural ministry.

- The Bible is full of the craziest miracles. Through Jesus it is possible to see all of these miracles in our own life as well!!

- Raise your hand if you can tell me some of the miracles Jesus did in the Bible.

Allow 3-5 children to share.

- Yes, that's right! He multiplied food to feed five thousand people, raised the dead, healed the sick, and set a lot of people free!

- If I remember correctly, I think Bobbie Baker has something to say about this! Bobbie, come on out!

- Today we are going to learn how to show other people how much Jesus was supernatural, and we get to be too.

- Now who is ready to see Bobbie?

- Bobbie, come on out!!

BOBBIE BAKER 5 minutes

Bobbie will help break down the kingdom core value and make the learning process fun and engaging. *This is where you will have your "own" Bobbie come out or start the video.*

BOBBIE LIVE

Bobbie will enter eating a rainbow lollipop.

- **Q: What did the salt say to the sugar?**

- **A: What's shakin', Sweetie?**

Have a jar of sugar for this part or something really sweet!

- **How many of you like sugar?!**

Allow children to answer.

- **Me too! How many of you know something is going to taste good if it has sugar in it?**

- **Well the supernatural is kinda like sugar.**

BOBBIE BAKER (continued)

- When we talk to someone who has never met God before, and when we partner with God as He does things we can't naturally do like prophesy or healing, it's supernatural!

- Let me read you a story from the recipe book.

- In Matthew 8:2-3 (NCV) it says, "Then a man with a skin disease came to Jesus. The man bowed down before him and said, 'Lord, you can heal me if you will.' Jesus reached out his hand and touched the man and said, 'I will. Be healed!' And immediately the man was healed from his disease."

- That man was healed just by the words he said! WOW!

- Because Jesus is behind the supernatural, He makes a whole situation "taste better" just like sugar does.

- When we as Christians remember that Holy Spirit is in us and full of power and love, we get to see all kinds of crazy miracles. Isn't that awesome?

- Thank you for stopping by my kitchen again, it is always a great time!

ACTIVATION: ROOTED IN LOVE
10 minutes

GOAL

Help the children remember that the purpose of the supernatural is helping people fall in love with Jesus. The children are powerful and don't have to wait until they are adults.

TEACHER

Well, we have a simple tool to help you listen to God. Get comfortable on the floor and close your eyes.

- This week we're going to be talking about how Jesus empowers supernatural ministry.
- Do you know that Jesus did everything out of love, and now we are empowered by Him to take risks and step out in the supernatural.
- The heart behind all supernatural ministry and evangelism should

ACTIVATION: ROOTED IN LOVE
(continued)

be love at all times.

- If we pray out of genuine love, people will be able to tell that we are seriously in love with Jesus.
- We should invite people to trust Jesus out of love, so that people will see that we mean what we say.
- We're not doing it because we HAVE too. Instead we're just telling them about our friendship with Jesus, and how much God loves us!
- We want you to practice partnering with the Holy Spirit to bring heaven to earth.
- We have a dice here. Whatever number you land on will have a different supernatural activity that goes with it.
- We are going to help you do this, so don't be nervous if you have never done this before.

ROLLING A 1: SING A PROPHETIC SONG

Have the child who rolls this number ask for a few words from God, and then sing those words over whomever they choose from the remaining children in the room.

ROLLING A 2: GIVE A PROPHETIC WORD USING AN ANIMAL

Have the child who rolls this number ask the Holy Spirit to show them an animal for another child in the room. They will give a word based on that animal.

EXAMPLE: God showed me a lion for you, and He wants you to know you are so powerful.

ROLLING A 3: PRAY FOR HEALING FOR SOMEONE IN YOUR ROOM

Have a child come up who needs healing. Have the child ask them what their pain level is out of ten:

- 0 - nothing hurts
- 10 - a lot of pain

Have the child pray, and then ask the child receiving healing where their pain level is at. If it is anything other than 0, pray again.

ROLLING A 4: SHARE A WORD OF KNOWLEDGE

Have the child that comes up ask the Holy Spirit for one detail about another child's life they could only know if they were asking Holy Spirit.

EXAMPLE: Something in the child's bedroom, their favorite stuffed animal, how many siblings they have, etc.

ACTIVATION: ROOTED IN LOVE
(continued)

ROLLING A 5: SHARE A TESTIMONY

Have the child who rolls this number share a story of a time where they have seen God show up in their life or someone else's life.

ROLLING A 6: WILD CARD

Have the child who rolls this number choose any of the other five activations to do.

To end this activation, have the children share how it went. Find out if this felt easy or hard for them, and if they realized that they could hear God even better than they thought.

TICKET TIMER 5 minutes

See Lesson Overview on page 12.

Building anticipation to this moment by celebrating each winner will make these few moments a lot of fun.

Have your container that is holding tickets, a ticket timer ready and have the children pull out their tickets. From the container, take out one ticket at a time, and read it until a winner is identified.

END GAME: NIGHT AT THE MUSEUM
25 minutes

This is a really fun time and something to look forward to at the end of each service. The goal here is fun! Children thrive when fun is just as much a priority as other parts of a lesson.

Choose a security guard (adult leader or trusted child), and statues (the rest of the children in the room). Assign a designated "out" area (a wall works great).

END GAME: NIGHT AT THE MUSEUM
(continued)

The security guard closes his/her eyes and counts down from ten, while the statues pose like statues. After the security guard reaches zero, he/she opens his/her eyes and studies the statues.

The statues may move at any time, but if the security guard sees them move (body movement, not breathing or blinking), then they are out. The goal of this game is to be the last standing statue.

If a player is the last statue standing, they become the security guard, and the game begins again with all the players.

During game play, the statues are required to move at least a little bit. If a player does not move for an extended period of time (three to five minutes), then they are given thirty seconds to make a movement, or they are out.

If the last few players are too hard to get out, increase the difficulty by including facial movements and blinking.

GOODBYE

When children are leaving for the day, take time to connect with the parents and tell them something good that happened with their child during the service.

(See next page for space to write lesson notes)

LESSON 9 NOTES

Lesson 10
His Kingdom Is Advancing

Main Themes

There is power in the Gospel and throughout God's kingdom! The children are world-changers and part of the good things God is doing in our country and around the world.

Supply List for Every Lesson

- ☐ Carnival tickets
- ☐ Container (baker's hat) for tickets
- ☐ Folder with Bible memorization charts
- ☐ Blank memorization charts for new kids
- ☐ Stickers for chart completion
- ☐ Two-minute ticket timer
- ☐ Bobbie Baker video and something to the play the video
  Or
- ☐ Live Skit with Bobbie's costume and props

Supply List for Lesson 10

- ☐ Bag filled with "get to know you" questions
- ☐ Thirty-second timer device
- ☐ Written (or printed) verse on large paper
- ☐ Written verse phrases on index cards (one set for each group of children)
- ☐ Soft worship music (best without words)
- ☐ Videos of fainting goats to share with children (to inspire)
- ☐ Bobbie Baker props (if doing live skit)
  - ☐ Chef hat
  - ☐ Mustache
  - ☐ Apron
  - ☐ Recipe book "Bible"
  - ☐ Bag of flour
  - ☐ Cupcake for Bobbie to eat

CONNECT TIME 10 minutes

Have a bag filled with silly "get to know you" questions. Count down from ten and pass the bag in a circle. When you get to zero, the person it lands on has to reach their hand in the bag to pull out a question and answer the question.

Here are some possible questions to get you started:
- Would you rather have a cat that sounds like a dog or a talking spider who only told jokes?
- If you were an avocado, what would be your favorite thing to do in the summer?
- If you had to eat one food for the rest of your life, what would it be?
- If you found a butterfly made of gold, what would you do?
- Would you rather have two left feet or three hands but the third hand was on your elbow?

If a child has already answered a specific question, feel free to have them choose a different question to answer.

BIBLE MEMORIZATION 30 minutes

John 3:3

What I'm about to tell you is true. No one can see God's kingdom unless they are born again. (NIRV)

GAME: BIBLE VERSE SCRAMBLE
30 minutes

TEACHER
- Have the verse printed out or written out on a piece of paper, large enough for children to read (8.5 inch X 11 inch).
- Write the verse out into sections on index cards, and have the children put them in the right order by looking at the verse on the wall. Once they are in order, have the children say the verse out loud and then mix them up one more time for them to put back in order.

GAME: BIBLE VERSE SCRAMBLE
(continued)

- Once the children think they know the verse, they can go to the designated leader to share.
- If they remember the verse, give them the prize, and if they have forgotten, have the child return to the group to practice the verse.
  - This is also the time where they get to put their sticker on their Bible memorization chart when they have memorized the verse.

TEACHING INTRO 5 minutes

- Today we're learning about how God's kingdom is advancing!
- Did you know His kingdom is ALWAYS advancing?
- The kingdom only has the ability to grow and expand!
- When Jesus died on the cross and won the battle over darkness, believers were filled with the Holy Spirit. Now we get to pray with power!
- Who can share a time with me when you felt powerful when you were praying.

Allow three to five children to share.

- Now, who is ready for Bobbie to come out and tell us more about this?

BOBBIE BAKER 5 minutes

Bobbie will help break down the kingdom core value and make the learning process fun and engaging. *This is where you will have your "own" Bobbie come out or start the video.*

(Continued on next page)

BOBBIE BAKER (continued)

- Hello and welcome back guys! It's joke time.

- Q: What gift can a baker give to his baker wife?

- A: A bouquet of flours.

Point to bag of flour.

- Oh…..not so many laughs this time…...that's okay……

- Anyways, do you guys know that the kingdom of God is like this bag of flour?

- When you use flour, it gets everywhere. When we partner with heaven, it can change everywhere we go.

- Watch this!

Bobbie will throw some flour in the air.

- Lets see what the recipe book says about this:

  - Ephesians 1:18-20 (NIRV) -I pray that you may understand more clearly. Then you will know the hope God has chosen you to receive. You will know that what God will give his holy people is rich and glorious. And you will know God's great power. It can't be compared with anything else. His power works for us who believe. It is the same mighty strength God showed. He showed this when he raised Christ from the dead. God seated him at his right hand in his heavenly kingdom.

- Who wants to bring the power and love of God to the people around them? Raise your hand!

- He actually wants to partner with us in bringing heaven to earth!

- That sounds amazing, but how do we partner with God to bring heaven to earth?

- What does it look like for us to advance God's kingdom?

Have a couple of children respond.

- Well, as a baker I can pray that all the people who eat my delicious cupcakes will experience the love of God and have a hunger for more of Him. I get to share about the love of Jesus any time I talk to one of my customers!

- Well, that is all for today! All this talk about the gospel has made me hungry again. Bye for now!

ACTIVATION: SHARING JESUS WITH OTHERS 10 minutes

GOAL

Connect the children to Jesus and have Him show them the people who need more of Him in their lives.

TEACHER

So now, we're going to do an activation and ask God to show us some things that we can do with Him to bring heaven to earth in our everyday lives!

SETUP

- Dim the lights.
- Have some soft music playing digitally or by a live musician.
- Have all the children find a quiet place by themselves in the room, and lay down on their backs with their hands over their hearts and eyes closed.

ENCOUNTER

- **I want you to picture Jesus and when you see Him, I want you to give me a thumbs up.**

- **Now ask Jesus, "Jesus, please show me people who need more of You that You want me to bring the kingdom of Heaven to."**

- **Jesus could show you someone in your family, in your own life, a relationship with a friend, maybe someone at school. Give me a thumbs up when you see what Jesus is showing you.**

Have children that want to share tell what they saw with the room.

TICKET TIMER 5 minutes

See Lesson Overview on page 12.

Building anticipation to this moment by celebrating each winner will make these few moments a lot of fun.

Have your container that is holding tickets, a ticket timer ready and have the children pull out their tickets. From the container, take out one ticket at a time, and read it until a winner is identified.

END GAME: FAINTING GOATS
25 minutes

This is a really fun time and something to look forward to at the end of each service. The goal here is fun! Children thrive when fun is just as much a priority as other parts of a lesson.

Before playing this game, look up some videos online of fainting goats to show your children. Children cannot run in this game but have to speed walk. Speed walking means that one foot has to be on the ground at a time otherwise it is running.

One person is chosen as the shepherd. Whoever the shepherd touches becomes the new shepherd.

The goats can fall to the ground to avoid being tagged for up to ten seconds. As long as they are on the ground, they are safe. The goat can't fall to the ground unless the shepherd is ten feet away or closer.

NOTE: This game is very tiring.

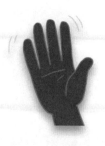

GOODBYE

When children are leaving for the day, take time to connect with the parents and tell them something good that happened with their child during the service.

LESSON 10 NOTES

Lesson 11
Free and Responsible

Main Themes

For this lesson the children will learn about the responsibility they have to live pure and holy in the freedom Jesus paid for on the cross.

Supply List for Every Lesson

- ☐ Carnival tickets
- ☐ Container (baker's hat) for tickets
- ☐ Folder with Bible memorization charts
- ☐ Blank memorization charts for new kids
- ☐ Stickers for chart completion
- ☐ Two-minute ticket timer
- ☐ Bobbie Baker video and something to the play the video
  Or
- ☐ Live Skit with Bobbie's costume and props

Supply List for Lesson 11

- ☐ Paper for paper airplanes
- ☐ Coloring utensils
- ☐ Way to display verse for all to read out loud in unison
- ☐ Bobbie Baker props (if doing live skit):
  - ☐ Chef hat
  - ☐ Mustache
  - ☐ Apron
  - ☐ Recipe book "Bible"
  - ☐ Spices
  - ☐ Pepper shaker
  - ☐ Jalapeño pepper for Bobbie to eat

CONNECT TIME: PAPER AIRPLANE COMPETITION 10 minutes

Have children make paper airplanes during this time, and provide markers for them to decorate them. Explain that they cannot throw them until the competition, or they will be disqualified.

At the end of connect time, have all those who would like to participate in the competition take their planes and stand on one side of the room. When you say go, have them throw their airplanes at one time. Whoever's plane goes the farthest will win!

BIBLE MEMORIZATION 30 minutes

Romans 8:1-2

Those who belong to Christ Jesus are no longer under God's judgment. Because of what Christ Jesus has done, you are free. You are now controlled by the law of the Holy Spirit who gives you life. The law of the Spirit frees you from the law of sin that brings death. (NIRV)

GAME: SILLY VOICES 30 minutes

- Display the verse large enough for all children to read on a paper or on a screen in your room. Have them read it in the following silly voices.
  - Read the verse through like a pirate.
  - Read the verse through like a man with a really deep voice.
  - Read the verse through like you have sucked in a lot of helium.
  - Read the verse through with a really strong southern accent.

GAME: SILLY VOICES (continued)

- Once the children think they know the verse, they can go to the designated leader to share.
- If they remember the verse, give them the prize, and if they have forgotten, have the child return to the group to practice the verse.
    - This is also the time where they get to put their sticker on their Bible memorization chart when they have memorized the verse.

TEACHING INTRO 5 minutes

- **Welcome to another day of kingdom core values!**
- **Do you know we have now learned a total of nine kingdom core values. Wow. Even looking at you, I can tell so much has changed.**
- **Raise your hand if you feel like something has changed in you since the first time we talked about kingdom core values.**

Allow three to five children to answer.

- **That's amazing. Well today we are going to talk about the kingdom core value: fFree and Responsible. When Jesus died on the cross, He did so to make us free from sin and death. With this freedom we are still responsible for the choices we make, but God will help us!**
- **What if I gave you a giant bag of cookies that had one hundred of your favorite cookies in it, and I told you that you are free to eat as many of them as you want. But what if I also told you that if you ate more than five of them, it could make you sick. What would you do?**

Allow the children to answer.

- **What would happen if you ate all one hundred.**

Allow the children to answer.

- **Yes, you would feel very sick.**
- **In life we need to have our self control be as large as our freedom.**
- **When we can learn to be powerful in our freedom, we can change the world.**

TEACHING INTRO (continued)

- This is another reason why Jesus died on the cross.
- Just like in the verse you memorized today, it says He died to set you free.
- Now, let's welcome Bobbie!

BOBBIE BAKER 5 minutes

Bobbie will help break down the kingdom core value and make the learning process fun and engaging. *This is where you will have your "own" Bobbie come out or start the video.*

BOBBIE LIVE

Bobbie will enter eating a pepper.

- Hello guys, I love it every time you join me in my kitchen!
- Wow! This pepper is spicy!
- Sharing with all of you my secret kingdom core value recipes is one of my favorite things in the whole world.
- I think I am sweating from how hot this pepper is!
- Anyways, it's joke time:
- Q: Why do fish swim in salt water?
- A: Because pepper makes them sneeze.
- Do you guys know that pepper is a spice?
- Do you know that when you are baking you get to choose which spices you use?
- Some spices are really good in baking cookies and cakes, like cinnamon and cocoa.
- There are also some spices that I would never want to choose for my baking sweets like super hot chili pepper or garlic or curry powder.
- Being free and responsible is kind of like choosing spices for your baking.
- You could choose bad spices for your cookies, and you wouldn't want to eat them. No one else would either!

BOBBIE BAKER (continued)

- If you make bad choices, God is not going to change the way He loves you, and He will help you make better choices in the future.

- If you choose spices that are good or make good choices, the world around you will likely change for the better, and I know your life will too!

- How many of you would actually try a cookie I made with all of the worst spices in it, raise your hand.

Pause to allow children to raise their hands.

- HAHA, that's amazing! You are all so brave. See you later!

ACTIVATION: HITTING THE RESET BUTTON 10 minutes

GOAL

Bring the children back into alignment with heaven if there are any areas of their lives they feel are not as good as they could be.

TEACHER

- How many of you after hearing about being free and responsible want to hit a giant "reset" button on your life because maybe you used freedom in a selfish way?

- Maybe there were times where you were given a lot of freedom and you took advantage of it? Maybe you didn't tell the full truth in a situation, or maybe it is just time to make better choices everywhere in your life?

- If that is you, we want to pray for you. Raise your hand if you want today to be the day that everything gets a fresh start so you can start making choices with powerful freedom in your minds.

When praying, lay hands on the children wanting prayer and make sure you follow Holy Spirit on what to pray. It could sound something like this:

- "Holy Spirit, today is the day that we start using the freedom You gave us in an even more powerful way."

- "From now on, we are going to bring Your voice into

ACTIVATION: HITTING THE RESET BUTTON (continued)

> situations where we feel like we don't know how to make the right choices."
> - "Holy Spirit, give us the power to know how to act in every situation. Thank You that You are for us and love us even in the moments where we wish we made different choices. Amen"
> - Who would like so share how you were feeling before we prayed and how you are feeling now?
>
> Allow 3-5 children to share.
> - Great job being so brave and open everyone! Now pull out your tickets, it is ticket timer time!

TICKET TIMER 5 minutes

See Lesson Overview on page 12.

Building anticipation to this moment by celebrating each winner will make these few moments a lot of fun.

Have your container that is holding tickets, a ticket timer ready and have the children pull out their tickets. From the container, take out one ticket at a time, and read it until a winner is identified.

END GAME: MR. FOX 25 minutes

This is a really fun time and something to look forward to at the end of each service. The goal here is fun! Children thrive when fun is just as much a priority as other parts of a lesson.

Choose one child to be Mr. Fox. Have all of the other players line up on the other side of the room you are playing in. Have Mr. Fox face away from the other children playing so they cannot single out specific players to get them out.

END GAME: MR. FOX (continued)

- Together, all the players call out, "What time is it, Mr. Fox?"

  - Mr. Fox responds by saying a time that is on the clock.
    Example: 1 o'clock - 12 o'clock.

  - The group then takes that many steps:

    - 1 o'clock would be one step

    - 2 o'clock would be two steps, etc.

- When, the caller playing Mr. Fox is ready, he/she can call out, "dinner time."

  - At this point Mr. Fox turns around and will chase the players to tag as many as possible.

  - If tagged, the players will have go sit in Mr. Fox's pot. To avoid being tagged, players must touch the wall of the starting place.

- On the next turn, players must avoid being tagged by Mr. Fox, and tag their friends out of the pot when they are close enough.

- Play until there is only one player left. This player can become Mr. Fox for the next round.

GOODBYE

When children are leaving for the day, take time to connect with the parents and tell them something good that happened with their child during the service.

(See next page for space to write lesson notes)

LESSON 11 NOTES

Lesson 12
Honor Affirms Value

Main Themes

For this lesson, the emphasis is on learning about a culture of honor and how it changes the way we live our lives.

Supply List for Every Lesson

☐ Carnival tickets
☐ Container (baker's hat) for tickets
☐ Folder with Bible memorization charts
☐ Blank memorization charts for new kids
☐ Stickers for chart completion
☐ Two-minute ticket timer
☐ Bobbie Baker video and something to the play the video
Or
☐ Live Skit with Bobbie's costume and props

Supply List for Lesson 12

☐ Ball to throw
☐ Copies of Romans 12:10 word search
☐ Writing utensils
☐ Paper
☐ Tape
☐ Markers
☐ Bobbie Baker props (if doing live skit):
  ☐ Chef hat
  ☐ Mustache
  ☐ Apron
  ☐ Recipe book "Bible"
  ☐ Vanilla
  ☐ Vanilla ice cream

CONNECT TIME: SILENT BALL
10 minutes

Have all the players begin by standing in a circle. Whoever is leading will be the only one who can speak. The leader is the only one who can decide who is out. Begin by throwing the ball to any player in the circle. Once the other player catches the ball they may then throw the ball to any other player in the circle. The game continues in this fashion until every player is out.

Ways to get out:

● If a player throws the ball too hard, too high, or too low for the receiving player to catch. The leader decides on whether or not the ball was catchable.

● If a player throws a ball to the receiver and the receiver drops the ball, the receiver is out.

● If any player talks or makes any noise.

BIBLE MEMORIZATION 30 minutes

Romans 12:10

Love one another deeply. Honor others more than yourselves. (NIRV)

GAME: SCRIPTURE WORD SEARCH
30 minutes

● The children will complete the word search puzzle found in the Appendix and then memorize the verse.

● Once the children think they know the verse, they can go to the designated leader to share.

● If they remember the verse, give them the prize, and if they have forgotten, have the child return to the group to practice the verse.

  ● This is also the time where they get to put their sticker on their Bible memorization chart when they have memorized the verse.

TEACHING INTRO 5 minutes

TEACHER

- Everyone is valuable and worthy to be honored simply because they are loved by God and wonderfully made.

- Jesus actually said that when we honor and love others, it is like we are doing it to Him too.

- It's that important to God! We have Christ inside us!

- Sometimes honoring is easy, but other times it is more challenging, especially when someone's actions do not line up with who they were made to be.

- Even in those moments we need to show honor with what we do and what we say. When we honor God this way, a lot of times we see people who are not being honoring want to follow our lead and be honoring too.

- It can teach others around us how to look like Jesus too.

- Well, now it is time to welcome in Bobbie! What do you think he will be eating today?

Allow the children to answer.

- Let's chant his name for him to come out! BOBBIE, BOBBIE, BOBBIE!

BOBBIE BAKER 5 minutes

Bobbie will help break down the kingdom core value and make the learning process fun and engaging. *This is where you will have your "own" Bobbie come out or start the video.*

(Continued on next page)

BOBBIE BAKER (continued)

BOBBIE LIVE

Bobbie will enter eating vanilla ice cream cone.

- Hey, guys. Who is ready for a joke?
- Q: What's a monkey's favorite ice cream flavor?
- A: Vanilla gorilla.
- Do you guys know what vanilla is?
- It is an ingredient that changes the flavor of recipes.
- If you leave vanilla out of a cookie or a cake, it does not taste right.
- Honor is like vanilla because when we have honor in our relationships, the relationships taste right. I mean are right. Hahaha.
- When we honor people, we feel different about all of the ways we interact with them.
- I once had this other baker that I could not stand and he made me so mad.
- I made a conscious choice to be loving and honoring to him, and now he and I are best friends. We share our best recipes with each other.
- Okay, bye. I have some cookies waiting for me that I need to eat.

ACTIVATION: HONOR IN ACTION
10 minutes

GOAL
Teach children a practical way to honor others, using words.

TEACHER
- Now we are going to honor each other! You guys actually know each other so this should be easy.
- We are going to take some time, and you get to honor each other by using our words.

- We have some paper, and we are going to tape it to all of your backs. You guys are going to walk around and write on each other's papers.
- If writing is hard for you, I want you to draw a quick picture instead.
- We don't want you to just talk about their outfit, or how their hair looks today; but rather honor something about who they are and their character.
- It can be something you have seen about who they are, or something you love about them.
- I will show you what I mean.

Pick someone from the room, tape the paper to their back, and write something nice about who they are. Then read it to the children and ask the person you chose how it made them feel.

- God has a lot that He loves about every single one of you. You are just getting to partner with Him in delivering the message!
- Have them write on the paper of at least two to three other children.

TICKET TIMER 5 minutes

See Lesson Overview on page 12.

Building anticipation to this moment by celebrating each winner will make these few moments a lot of fun.

Have your container that is holding tickets, a ticket timer ready and have the children pull out their tickets. From the container, take out one ticket at a time, and read it until a winner is identified.

END GAME: FOUR CORNERS 25 minutes

This is a really fun time and something to look forward to at the end of each service. The goal here is fun! Children thrive when fun is just as much a priority as other parts of a lesson.

Explain the rules to the children. Have four preset corners; these could be actual corners in the room, or specific areas in the room that would stand out as four separate areas. Also designate an "out" area; a wall would work perfectly for the out area.

To begin the game, have a Caller who is an adult leader or trusted child.

The caller must then close their eyes, count down from ten, and spin in a circle. While this is happening the players select one of the four corners as their own, and go to it. The children must move as quietly as possible so the caller does not know which corner is full of people. Once the caller reaches zero, they call out a corner (1, 2, 3, or 4).

The players in the corresponding corner are then considered out and need to go to the designated out area. The last player standing is the winner and can become the new caller.

NOTE: If there are a lot of players that try to change their corner once the caller has reached zero, you may include the following rule. If you move to a different corner after the caller reaches zero, you are immediately out.

GOODBYE

When children are leaving for the day, take time to connect with the parents and tell them something good that happened with their child during the service.

LESSON 12 NOTES

Lesson 13
Generous like Our Father

Main Themes

This lesson is all about how generous God is and what it looks like to be generous.

Supply List for Every Lesson

- ☐ Carnival tickets
- ☐ Container (baker's hat) for tickets
- ☐ Folder with Bible memorization charts
- ☐ Blank memorization charts for new kids
- ☐ Stickers for chart completion
- ☐ Two-minute ticket timer
- ☐ Bobbie Baker video and something to the play the video
  Or
- ☐ Live Skit with Bobbie's costume and props

Supply List for Lesson 13

- ☐ Ball or object to throw
- ☐ Written or printed verse on large paper
- ☐ Videos of fainting goats to share with children (to inspire)
- ☐ Bobbie Baker props (if doing live skit):
  - ☐ Chef hat
  - ☐ Mustache
  - ☐ Apron
  - ☐ Recipe book "Bible"
  - ☐ Baking soda
  - ☐ Acts 20:35 written for Recipe book "Bible"
  - ☐ Golden chocolate coins

CONNECT TIME: SILENT BALL
10 minutes

Have the children learn more about each other by standing in a circle and throwing a ball or object to each other across the circle.

When children catch it, they either have to tell one fact about themselves, share the grossest thing they have ever eaten, or tell a joke/riddle.

If the children have all gone once and you want the game to keep going, you can have them share the name of their favorite pet or a pet they want to own one day.

To make the game harder, have the children stand on one foot or jump on one foot while they play.

BIBLE MEMORIZATION 30 minutes

Philippians 4:19

My God will meet all your needs. He will meet them in keeping with his wonderful riches. These riches come to you because you belong to Christ Jesus. (NIRV)

GAME: WATCH THE BALL 30 minutes

- Have the verse written or printed out on a piece of paper, and have it on a wall nearby that the children can read.
- Hold a ball in front of the children. Tell them that when you raise the ball, they need to yell the verse. When you lower the ball, they must whisper the verse.

GAME: WATCH THE BALL (continued)

- When you hold the object to your right, the children have to say the verse super fast, and when you hold the object to your left, the children have to say the verse super slow.
- Repeat the different positions a few times until the children memorize the verse completely.
- If they remember the verse, give them the prize and if they have forgotten, have the child return to the group to practice the verse.
  - This is also the time where they get to put their sticker on their Bible memorization chart.

TEACHING INTRO 5 minutes

- **Hey guys! This week, we're learning about the kingdom core value: Generous like Our Father!**
- **When we say father we are talking about our Father in heaven, God.**
- **But first we have a few questions for you guys, to see what you think before we start this.**
- **What does generosity mean to you?**

Allow two to three children to answer.

- **What are ways that you have seen Father God be generous?**

Allow two to three children to answer.

- **Why is it important to be generous?**

Allow two to three children to answer.

- **Can you think of a story in the Bible where God was generous?**

Allow two to three children to answer.

- **Yeah, those were all really great answers. Do you know what the most generous thing God did for us?**

Allow two to three children to answer.

- **Yes! He gave His one and only Son to us, and then He laid down His life for us!**

BOBBIE BAKER 5 minutes

Bobbie will help break down the kingdom core value and make the learning process fun and engaging. *This is where you will have your "own" Bobbie come out or start the video.*

BOBBIE LIVE

Bobbie will enter eating a handful of chocolate coins.

- Welcome back to my kitchen everybody.

- Can you guys see what I am eating?

Pause for children to say what they think it is.

- That's right! Chocolate that looks like money!

- We are learning about how generous God is, and one way to be generous is to give money away to someone.

- So I thought I would eat some chocolate money! Haha!

- Now, it's joke time:

- Q: What kind of drink do they sell at bakeries?

- A: Baking soda.

- Let me read you something from my recipe book. Acts 20:35 (NIRV) says, "Remember the words of Jesus. He said, 'It is more blessed to give than to receive.'"

- Can you guys believe that? How many have you have ever baked something and gave it to someone else? Isn't it just the best to give to others?

Allow children to answer.

- I wish I could do it every day!

- When you bake with baking soda, it makes whatever you are making expand. When you add generosity into moments with people, it makes other people's hearts expand with love.

- When you are baking and the recipe says to be generous with something, it means use it a lot. We have access to the kingdom, and in the kingdom there is always more than enough!

- Next week will be your last week in my kitchen!

ACTIVATION: REMEMBERING GOD'S GENEROSITY 10 minutes

GOAL

Teach the children the power that thankfulness has in their lives and their families' lives.

TEACHER

- **Generosity is a mindset, and it's not just about money. There are a lot of different kinds of wealth. There is time, money, acts of kindness, and other things.**
- **Jesus was generous with love toward us and because we received from Him first, it is easier to know how to do this with others.**
- **Now I want to share a testimony of a time when I have seen God's generosity.**

Share a testimony from your own life that shows God's generosity.

ENCOUNTER

- **Now we are going to do an encounter!**

We will take the children on an encounter with Jesus where they reflect on ways in which God has been generous to their family. Then we will have the children respond to gratitude within this encounter. At the end, have the children share what they felt during that encounter. They reason we have them share is so that we can really feel the generosity that is happening in each other's lives.

Follow these steps:

- Have children find a spot in the room where they will not be disturbed.
- Have children lay flat on their back, put their hands on their hearts and close their eyes.
- **With your eyes closed I want you to picture Jesus and take His hand.**
- **As soon as you have His hand, can you raise your hand to show me?**
- **Now, I want you to look into Jesus' eyes and say, "Jesus, remind me of all the ways that you have been generous to me or have given to me, my family or friends."**

ACTIVATION: HITTING THE RESET BUTTON (continued)

- **When you see some of those moments, put your hand up.**
- **Now if you would like to share, raise your hand.**

Allow time for the children to share.

TICKET TIMER 5 minutes

See Lesson Overview on page 12.

Building anticipation to this moment by celebrating each winner will make these few moments a lot of fun.

Have your container that is holding tickets, a ticket timer ready and have the children pull out their tickets. From the container, take out one ticket at a time, and read it until a winner is identified.

END GAME: NIGHT AT THE MUSEUM 25 minutes

This is a really fun time and something to look forward to at the end of each service. The goal here is fun! Children thrive when fun is just as much a priority as other parts of a lesson.

Choose a security guard (adult leader or trusted child), and statues (the rest of the children in the room). Assign a designated "out" area (a wall works great).

The security guard closes his/her eyes and counts down from ten, while the statues pose like statues. After the security guard reaches zero, he/she opens his/her eyes and studies the statues.

END GAME: NIGHT AT THE MUSEUM
(continued)

The statues may move at any time, but if the security guard sees them move (body movement, not breathing or blinking), then they are out. The goal of this game is to be the last standing statue.

If a player is the last statue standing, they become the security guard, and the game begins again with all the players.

During game play, the statues are required to move at least a little bit. If a player does not move for an extended period of time (three to five minutes), then they are given thirty seconds to make a movement, or they are out.

If the last few players are too hard to get out, increase the difficulty by including facial movements and blinking.

GOODBYE

When children are leaving for the day, take time to connect with the parents and tell them something good that happened with their child during the service.

(See next page for space to write lesson notes)

LESSON 13 NOTES

Lesson 14
Hope in a Glorious Church

Main Themes
In this final lesson, the children will learn that God has great plans in store for them and the church!

Supply List for Every Lesson

☐ Carnival tickets
☐ Container (baker's hat) for tickets
☐ Folder with Bible memorization charts
☐ Blank memorization charts for new kids
☐ Stickers for chart completion
☐ Two-minute ticket timer
☐ Bobbie Baker video and something to the play the video
Or
☐ Live Skit with Bobbie's costume and props

Supply List for Lesson 14

☐ Copies of fruit handout found in the Appendix.
☐ Coloring utensils
☐ Soft worship music (ideally songs without words)
☐ Videos of fainting goats to share with children (to inspire)
☐ Bobbie Baker props (if doing live skit):
  ☐ Chef hat
  ☐ Mustache
  ☐ Apron
  ☐ Recipe book "Bible"
  ☐ Cupcake
  ☐ Banana labeled "joy"
  ☐ Apple labeled "self-control"
  ☐ Strawberries

CONNECT TIME 10 minutes

Have children sit in a circle and share testimonies from this series, favorite things that Bobbie Baker did, or areas in their life that they would like prayer for.

Lead children to pray for specific areas of breakthrough for these people. If children share they want prayer for healing, always follow up with prayer. Then make sure to dialogue, asking if they have been healed or if the problem area has improved at all.

BIBLE MEMORIZATION 30 minutes

Galatians 5:22-23

But the fruit the Holy Spirit produces is love, joy and peace. It is being patient, kind and good. It is being faithful and gentle and having control of oneself. There is no law against things of that kind. (NIRV)

GAME: FRUIT BOWL 30 minutes

TEACHER
- Print and cut out the activity sheet from this lesson found in the Appendix, and allow the children to color in the fruits.
- When they have finished this, have them all stand in a circle holding one of the fruits.
- Start the game by yelling out: "But the fruit of the Spirit is…" followed by calling out where the verse is found in the Bible.
- Next you will call out one of the fruits of the Spirit: love, joy, peace, patience, ext. Children holding that fruit of the Spirit will run into the middle of the circle and switch places with one of the other children holding that same fruit of the Spirit as quickly as possible.

GAME: FRUIT BOWL (continued)

- Once the children think they know the verse, they can go to the designated leader to share.
- If they remember the verse, give them the prize, and if they have forgotten, have the child return to the group to practice the verse.
  - This is also the time where they get to put their sticker on their Bible memorization chart when they have memorized the verse.

NOTES

- If you only have a few children, make sure that two of every fruit is represented in the circle of children so that they have someone to switch places with.
- If you have a lot of children, print multiple sheets so that a fruit of the Spirit is represented multiple times.

TEACHING INTRO 5 minutes

- **Hey guys, today we are talking about our last kingdom core value which is: Hope in a Glorious Church.**
- **This core value means that we believe Christians are going to continue to become more and more like Jesus so that the world will see how amazing He is. Then they will and reach out for Him and His kingdom.**
- **God's kingdom is full of God's goodness, no loss, full of love, and sin does not exist; we as God's church are meant to bring this to every person we meet.**
- **We want to see God's perfect heart become real even in situations that feel difficult or have conflict.**

BOBBIE BAKER 5 minutes

Bobbie will help break down the kingdom core value and make the learning process fun and engaging. *This is where you will have your "own" Bobbie come out or start the video.*

BOBBIE LIVE

Bobbie will enter eating a cupcake.

- **Helllo! Can someone tell me what the kingdom core value for today is?**

Allow the children to answer.

- **Yes! Hope in a Glorious Church.**

- **I want to talk to you guys more about this, but first I want to tell you a joke!**

- **Q: What fruit teases you a lot?**

- **A: Ba na..na..na..na..naaaa**

Say it in a funny teasing way.

- **Hahahaha. Speaking of fruits, do you know that there are fruits of the Spirit?**

- **How many of them can you name?**

Allow the children to answer.

- **Yes, there is love, joy, peace, patience, kindness, goodness, gentleness, faithfulness and self-control.**

- **When we have these fruits of the Spirit in our lives, we can be part of God's Church that helps bring heaven to earth. Let me show you what I mean.**

Bobbie will have a few fruits that say the fruit of the Spirit on them.

- **If I take this joy banana and take a bite, watch what happens.**

Bobbie takes a bite and laughs out loud.

- **Now watch what happens when I take a bite of this self-control apple.**

Bobbie takes a bite.

- **Wow, all of the sudden I feel like I can say no to that chocolate cake that is in the fridge that I have already eaten 3 giant pieces of. I feel so in control of myself.**

- **When we partner with the Holy Spirit and all the good fruits that come from Him, we can change the world around us!**

- **I have loved getting to know you guys and after meeting you, I feel more inspired to make new recipes in my kitchen.**

- **I can't wait to see what I can create now that I have met you guys!**

- **Bye for now and keep cooking with kingdom core values!**

ACTIVATION: COMMISSIONING
10 minutes

GOAL

Leave the children marked by what they have learned about in this lesson series.

TEACHER

Play soft music as you introduce this part of the lesson, and also while you are doing the commissioning.

- **Now that you have learned about all of these incredible kingdom core values, we want to pray for you so that you can take this into the world long after we are done.**
- **In the Old Testament of the Bible, the part of the Bible when people like Abraham, Moses, and Queen Esther were around, oil was used to show the passing of the anointing/blessing.**
- **In the New Testament, the part of the Bible that speaks about people like Jesus and the 12 apostles, we see that the anointing of the Holy Spirit can now be passed through laying our hands on people because the anointing is inside of us:**
    - **1 John 2:27(NIRV) says, "But you have received the Holy Spirit from God. He continues to live in you."**
    - **Paul, in the Bible, also thought the impartation and laying hands on people was part of becoming fully secure in an area.**
    - **He longed to impart spiritual gifts to the Roman believers to give them a better foundation, " I long to see you. I want to make you strong by giving you a gift from the Holy Spirit." (Rom. 1:11 NIRV).**
- **So now, we as leaders, want to lay hands on you guys to seal what God has done in you over the last fourteen lessons.**
- **Think of it like licking an envelope to seal it. It keeps all the important things inside!**

Have children stand shoulder to shoulder with their hands palm side up, and lay hands on every child's shoulders individually as you pray. Be led by the Holy Spirit.

- **Example:**
    - **"God, thank you for <u>(insert name of child)</u>. I pray that as he/she gets older that he/she will know God better and better. We pray that You seal these kingdom core values in his/her life, and we declare that as he/she lives out these values, he/she will always be able to find You. Amen."**

TICKET TIMER 5 minutes

See Lesson Overview on page 12.

Building anticipation to this moment by celebrating each winner will make these few moments a lot of fun.

Have your container that is holding tickets, a ticket timer ready and have the children pull out their tickets. From the container, take out one ticket at a time, and read it until a winner is identified.

END GAME: FAINTING GOATS
25 minutes

This is a really fun time and something to look forward to at the end of each service. The goal here is fun! Children thrive when fun is just as much a priority as other parts of a lesson.

Before playing this game, look up some videos online of fainting goats to show your children. Children cannot run in this game but have to speed walk. Speed walking means that one foot has to be on the ground at a time otherwise it is running.

One person is chosen as the shepherd. Whoever the shepherd touches becomes the new shepherd.

The goats can fall to the ground to avoid being tagged for up to ten seconds. As long as they are on the ground, they are safe. The goat can't fall to the ground unless the shepherd is ten feet away or closer.

NOTE: This game is very tiring.

GOODBYE

When children are leaving for the day, take time to connect with the parents and tell them something good that happened with their child during the service.

LESSON 14 NOTES

Conclusion

We are excited that you partnered with us and Bobbie Baker! We look forward to hearing the testimonies of how God is moving and transforming you and your children! In our children's department, children are understanding the heart behind the lifestyle of being a Christian and have had powerful encounters where Holy Spirit came. Many of the children were on the floor worshiping Jesus for the rest of the service. We also have had the older children taking on a deep understanding of the kingdom core values. They now want to start leading and teaching their peers.

We now give them a few minutes to preach what we called a "sermonette" (mini sermon) to their peers, sharing their thoughts and personal testimonies about the core value themes. These children grew greatly in leadership, responsibility, and ownership of these core values from this exercise.

We pray that God continues to multiply our testimonies over you and your children. Remember, that there is always more!

Be on the lookout for more adventures with Bobbie Baker's friends.

We **love** testimonies and feedback! Please let us know how *Bobbie Baker* is impacting your children's ministry by emailing us at children@bethel.com

Appendix

Bobbie Baker's Best Brownies Recipe 124

Bible Memorization Chart 125

Bobbie Baker Coloring Pages (Lessons 3 & 9) 126

Family Crest (Lesson 6)............................. 131

Drawing the Verse Activity (Lesson 9)................132

Scripture Word Search (Lesson 12) 133

Fruit Bowl Activity Sheet (Lesson 14)................. 135

Bobbie Baker's Best Brownies

Ingredients

- ☐ ½ cup butter
- ☐ 1 cup white sugar
- ☐ 2 eggs
- ☐ 1 teaspoon vanilla extract
- ☐ ☐ cup unsweetened cocoa powder
- ☐ ½ cup all-purpose flour
- ☐ ¼ teaspoon salt
- ☐ ¼ teaspoon baking powder

Bobbie's Twist

- ☐ 1 measure of patience
- ☐ 3 giggles of joy
- ☐ 2 kisses of loving kindness
- ☐ 1 big prayer of faith, hope, and love for the people enjoying the brownies!

Frosting

- ☐ 3 tablespoons butter, softened
- ☐ 3 tablespoons unsweetened cocoa powder
- ☐ 1 tablespoon honey
- ☐ 1 teaspoon vanilla extract
- ☐ 1 cup confectioners' sugar
- ☐ Add all ingredients to list

Directions

1. Preheat oven to 350 degrees F (175 degrees C). Grease and flour an 8-inch square pan.
2. In a large saucepan, melt 1/2 cup butter. Remove from heat, and stir in sugar, eggs, and 1 teaspoon vanilla. Beat in 1/3 cup cocoa, 1/2 cup flour, salt, and baking powder.
3. Next is the special Bobbie ingredients. Add 1 measure of patience by pausing a moment, taking a deep breath, trusting the Lord, and breathing out slowly. Next, sprinkle in 3 giggles of joy and 2 kisses of loving kindness. Lastly, pray 1 big prayer of faith, hope, and love for the people that will eat these brownies.
4. Spread batter into prepared pan.
5. Bake in preheated oven for 25 to 30 minutes. Do not overcook.
6. To Make Frosting: Combine 3 tablespoons softened butter, 3 tablespoons cocoa, honey, 1 teaspoon vanilla extract, and 1 cup confectioners' sugar. Stir until smooth. Frost brownies while they are still warm.

Nutrition Facts

Per Serving: 183 calories; 9 g fat; 25.7 g carbohydrates; 1.8 g protein; 44 mg cholesterol; 110 mg sodium; unlimited love, joy, peace, patience, kindness, goodness, faithfulness, gentleness, and self-control in every Holy Spirit filled serving!

Recipe adapted from allrecipes.com

Kingdom Core Values
Bible Memorization Chart

Child's Name: _____

Core Value	Scripture	Date	☆
Intro Into Kingdom Core Values	John 3:16		
God is Good	Matthew 7:7		
Salvation Creates Joyful Identity	Romans 5:8		
Responsive to Grace	Ephesians 2:8-9		
Focused on His Presence	John 4:23		
Creating Healthy Family	Ephesians 1:5		
God's Word Transforms	Psalm 119:11		
God is Still Speaking	1 Corinthians 14:3		
Jesus Empowers Supernatural Ministry	1 Thessalonians 1:5		
His Kingdom is Advancing	John 3:3		
Free and Responsible	Romans 8:1-2		
Honor Affirms Value	Romans 12:10		
Generous Like My Father	Philippians 4:19		
Hope in a Glorious Church	Galatians 5:22-23		

Drawing the Verse

1 Thessalonians 1:5

Look up and write out the memory verse.
After you have written out the verse, memorize the scripture.

Draw a picture of what this verse means to you.

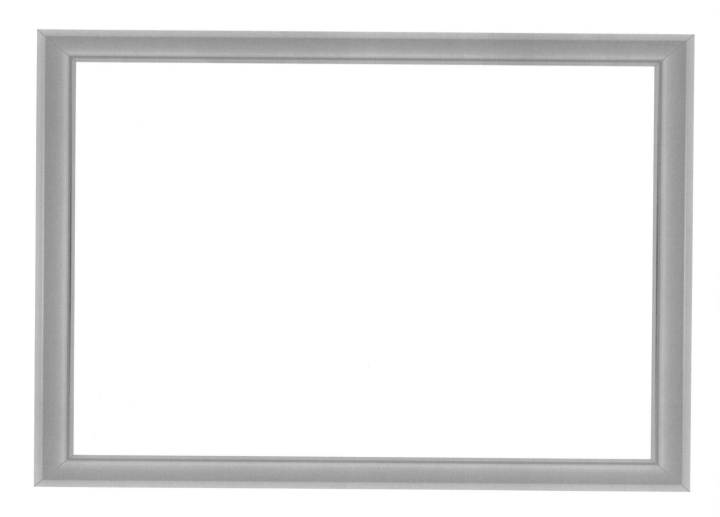

Romans 12:10 Word Search

O Y E A V E P U T L O R O E
S O O E T S T E R H N N E E
R O O U D R N S R E H N M
T R O N R E M H S E N A E
N M T N T S E N E H O S H V
M N H D T M E P Y D R L T O
A O E N S E L L W O M A L
E Y R R E M A T V Y S T E S
N T S E V L E W T E N N
M R R R E H T O N A S H E E
V O V R E H L E S R O N O H
N V R E S H O S N A M O R E
P T N E E V E T E O O O H M
N R Y E S H O N O R S O S O

Romans 12:10 Word Search Answers

LOVE
ONE
ANOTHER
DEEPLY
HONOR
OTHERS
MORE
THAN
YOURSELVES
ROMANS
TWELVE
TEN

LOVE	LOVE	GOODNESS	GOODNESS
JOY	JOY	FAITHFULNESS	FAITHFULNESS
PEACE	PEACE	GENTLENESS	GENTLENESS
PATIENCE	PATIENCE	SELF-CONTROL	SELF-CONTROL
KINDNESS	KINDNESS		

BOBBIE BAKER
CURRICULUM UPGRADES

Less *prep.*
More *fun.*

Give Sunday School a boost with **Curriculum Upgrades**

Additional Resources for Students, Teachers, and Families in Every Lesson

Increase engagement.
Cut down on prep time.

Curriculum Upgrades are multi-media resources that accompany each week's lesson. These tools have been specially developed to help leaders and students connect with God, parents, and each other in more meaningful ways – without extra additional planning. What are you waiting for? Upgrade Sunday School today!

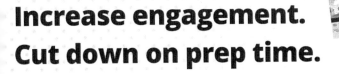

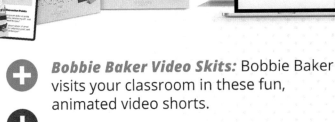

+ ***Bobbie Baker Video Skits:*** Bobbie Baker visits your classroom in these fun, animated video shorts.

+ ***Teacher's Training Videos:*** These brief weekly videos make lesson prep easier on volunteers while equipping them with vital tools for Kingdom children's ministry.

+ ***Take-Home Resources:*** Send students home with valuable Scripture memory tools, discussion prompts for parents, and fun Bible-based activities.

Upgrade Your Curriculum at
www.DestinyImage.co/bobbie-baker

Made in the USA
Middletown, DE
19 July 2022